OSPREY
PUBLISHING

Buffalo Soldiers 1892–1918

Ron Field • Illustrated by Richard Hook

Consultant editor Martin Windrow

First published in Great Britain in 2005 by Osprey Publishing,
Midland House, West Way, Botley, Oxford, OX2 0PH, UK
443 Park Avenue South, New York, NY 10016, USA
Email: info@ospreypublishing.com

ISBN 1 84176 898 7

Design: Ken Vail Graphic Design, Cambridge, UK
Index by Alison Worthington
Originated by The Electronic Page Company, Cwmbran, UK
Printed in China through World Print Ltd.

05 06 07 08 09   10 9 8 7 6 5 4 3 2 1

A CIP catalog record for this book is available from the British Library

FOR A CATALOG OF ALL BOOKS PUBLISHED BY OSPREY MILITARY
AND AVIATION PLEASE CONTACT:

North America:
Osprey Direct
2427 Bond Street, University Park, IL 60466, USA
Email: info@ospreydirectusa.com

All other regions:
Osprey Direct UK
PO Box 140, Wellingborough, Northants, NN8 2FA, UK
Email: info@ospreydirect.co.uk

Buy online at **www.ospreypublishing.com**

Acknowledgments

The author wishes to thank the following for their generous
assistance: Tim Phillips, Museum Director, Fort Huachuca
Museum; Peter Harrington, Curator, Anne S.K. Brown
Military Collection, Brown University; Clifton Hyatt, Curator
of Photography, United States Army Military History
Institute; Jessie Nunn, Archives Clerk, K.Ross Toole
Archives, Mike and Maureen Mansfield Library, The
University of Montana – Missoula; and Anne Clarkson,
Russell Wolfe, Larry Strayer, John P.Langelier, Roger
D.Cunningham, Anthony Gero, Dusan Farrington, and
Kurt Hughes.

Artist's Note

Readers may care to note that the original paintings from
which the color plates in this book were prepared are
available for private sale. All reproduction copyright
whatsoever is retained by the Publishers. All enquiries
should be addressed to:

Scorpio Gallery,
PO Box 475, Hailsham, East Sussex BN27 2SL, UK

The Publishers regret that they can enter into no
correspondence upon this matter.

BUFFALO SOLDIERS 1892–1918

INTRODUCTION

On August 18, 1918, Sgt William Butler, Company L, 369th Infantry, won the Distinguished Service Cross – the second highest award for bravery – and the French *Croix de Guerre* for breaking up a German raiding party in US trenches near Maison-de-Champagne. Armed with a Chauchat automatic rifle, Butler killed four of the raiders, captured six including an officer, and put the rest to flight. In this portrait Butler also displays a marksmanship badge, and two wound chevrons on his right forearm. (US National Archives)

The African-American soldier played an important part in the operations of the US Army during the so-called "age of American Imperialism" from 1898 to 1916, and two years later went on to distinguish himself in the trenches of World War I.

In the Spanish-American War of 1898, black troops charged fearlessly up Kettle Hill alongside Teddy Roosevelt and his Rough Riders. As conflict with the Spanish developed into the Philippine Insurrection, black Regulars and Volunteers became embroiled in the long drawn-out struggle with the Filipino nationalist forces and the dreaded Moro warriors of the island of Mindanao. In Mexico during 1916, black cavalrymen and infantry went on campaign against Mexican revolutionaries under Pancho Villa, and the former conducted the last US cavalry charge in battle at Aguas Calientes in April of that year.

With the involvement of US troops in World War I in 1917, soldiers of the African-American 92nd and 93rd Divisions saw combat in France; four regiments earned collective citations for the French *Croix de Guerre* for their outstanding bravery, while numerous individual soldiers won gallantry decorations including the Distinguished Service Cross. By the war's end, a total of 5,000 black soldiers had been wounded and 750 killed in the bitter fighting of the summer and fall of 1918. Every foe that encountered him – whether Spanish, Filipino, Mexican or German – learned to respect the bravery of the African-American "buffalo soldier."

CHRONOLOGY

1894 Coxey's Rebellion

1898 **Spanish-American War:**
June 8, Las Guásimas; June 21, Tayabacoa; July 1, El Caney, San Juan Hill & Kettle Hill; July 25, Yauco

1899 **Philippine Insurrection:**
October 6, Arayat; November 18, O'Donnell; December 7, Naguilian

1900 January 5, Camansi; January 6–7, Iba; July 4, Manacling; December 17, Tagbac

1906 July 24, Tabon-Tabon

1914 Mexican Border operations:
December 1914–January 1915, Naco
November 3–4, Agua Prieta

1916 Punitive Expedition:
April 1, Aguas Calientes; April 12, Santa Cruz de
Villegas; June 21, Carrizal

1918 World War I:
Aisne–Marne offensive: July 18–August 18, Butte de
Mesnil; August 30, Frapelle
St Mihiel offensive: September 21, Binarsville
Meuse–Argonne offensive: September 26,
Maison-en-Champagne; September 28, Hill 188,
Champagne Marne Sector; September 29,
Ardeuil & Sechault; October 1, Monthois

FRONTIER DUTIES, 1892–1898

Enlisted men of Co G, 25th Infantry, photographed at Fort Missoula, Montana, at some date before 1895 – note the chasseur-pattern 1889 forage cap. The man at left has a tan woven infantry cartridge belt, its 1887-pattern H-shaped "US" plate visible under his open jacket. (Elrod Collection, K.Ross Toole Archives, University of Montana – Missoula)

For eight years following the end of the Indian Wars in 1891, the four Regular regiments of buffalo soldiers continued to garrison various frontier posts and to police the tamed American West. The 9th Cavalry was headquartered at Fort Robinson, NE, throughout this period. The 10th Cavalry was based at Fort Assinniboine, MT, with troops also stationed at Fort Keogh. The 24th Infantry was in New Mexico with headquarters at Fort Bayard, but subsequently removed to Fort Douglas, UT, in October 1896. The 25th Infantry operated out of Fort Missoula, MT, and Fort Buford, ND, plus several other stations.

During this period African-American troops were often included among those used to bring under control the civil unrest caused by industrial strife. Early in 1892 a confrontation developed between the mine owners and labor unions in the Coeur d'Alene mining district of Idaho. Scenes of disorder and anarchy culminated on the Fourth of July with the American flag being riddled with bullets and spat and trampled upon by strikers; and by July 11 several mines had been blown up, with consequent loss of life. Federal aid was invoked, and Regular Army troops were quickly on their way to the area, including a provisional battalion from the 25th Infantry consisting of Companies F, G & H, commanded by Capt W.T.Sanborn. Although strikers blew up the tracks of the North Pacific Railroad, the buffalo soldiers finally managed to reach the troubled area via the Coeur d'Alene City, Harrison & Union Pacific Railroad on July 14. Making camp at Wardner Junction, they were immediately assigned to guarding trains, scouting, furnishing escorts and making arrests.

In April 1894, elements of the 25th Infantry and 10th Cavalry were among troops dispatched to intercept a train on the Montana & Pacific Railroad carrying members of "Coxey's Army," a group of unemployed workers led by Jacob Sechler Coxey, who were on their way to protest in Washington, DC.

The local press would subsequently comment on "the excellence of the negro as a soldier. During the entire period that the guard was on duty, no act of the troops was open to criticism, and there was not a single instance of an unjust exercise of authority." The *Army & Navy Journal* of August 25, 1894, stated that the railroad authorities were "naturally loud in their praise of the troops, and the majority of strikers admit that if the soldiers had to be called out there could have been none better than… the 25th Infantry." During July of that year, four companies of the 24th Infantry, plus two companies of the white 1st Cavalry, were assigned to guard mail trains on the Sante Fe Railroad.

In the summer of 1896 the entire 10th Cavalry was in the field rounding up Cree Indians under Little Bear, who had fled from their reservations in Canada and were committing minor depredations over the border in the USA. Large numbers of Cree were escorted back north and handed over to the Canadian authorities. One of the leaders of this assignment was Lt John J.Pershing, commanding Troop D. Later known as "Black Jack," the future commander of the American Expeditionary Force (AEF) acquired that nickname for earlier service with the 10th Cavalry.

In June 1897, the 10th Cavalry got a new commander when Col J.K.Mizner was promoted to brigadier-general, and Col Guy V.Henry took command. That same year, Troops A, E & K were called out to the Tongue River Indian Agency to resolve a disturbance among the Cheyenne. Thanks to the diplomacy of the officers, and respect among the Indians for their old adversaries, the buffalo soldiers made four arrests and the outbreak died down. At the end of 1897 the Army consolidated the 10th Cavalry at Forts Assinniboine and Keogh, where they remained until the outbreak of the Spanish-American War.

Bicycle trials, 1896

It was the Italian Bersaglieri light infantry who first used the bicycle for military purposes in 1875; and in 1891 the "push bike" made its first martial appearance in America when the Connecticut Militia formed a

Photographed in San Francisco c.1905, Capt Charles Young wears the 1902-pattern service uniform and cap. This remarkable man – a gifted linguist and musician, and a teacher when he sat the competitive examination for the Academy – was the first African-American to be commissioned in the US Army, graduating from West Point in 1889. Nine other black cadets were discharged one by one, leaving him alone and friendless to face bigotry and ostracism. During five years with the 9th Cavalry on the Frontier he earned great respect and affection from his men. In 1898 Maj Young trained the 9th Ohio Volunteer (Colored) Infantry, but they never got to Cuba; he had to revert to lieutenant's rank on returning to the 9th Cavalry. Captain Young led his troopers on Samar in the Philippines for 18 months from May 1901, and returned to the islands for another tour in 1908, after excelling as US military attaché to Haiti. In 1912–15 he was seconded to command forces in the ramshackle African-American republic of Liberia, West Africa, nearly dying from a bullet wound complicated by black water fever. See also the photograph on page 27. (USAHMI)

Signal Corps bicycle unit. Four years later, Gen Nelson A.Miles – a member of the League of Military Wheelmen – promoted the use of the bicycle for reconnaissance purposes in the Regular Army. By November 1895 the US Signal Corps had adopted it as a means of distributing telegraph and telephone wires. In 1896 a detachment of the 25th Infantry, commanded by Lt James A.Moss of Co F (and later CO of the 367th Infantry in World War I), was selected to conduct extensive trials of the bicycle in mountainous country.

During the following year Moss led his 21 men on a 1,900-mile journey from Fort Missoula, MT, to St Louis, MO. When a civilian asked one of the riders where they were going, the soldier replied, "The Lord only knows. We're following the Lieutenant." Taking 41 days, the buffalo soldiers rode through heat, snow and rain, and successfully proved the practicality of military cycling. Their mounts were 32lb Spaulding safety bicycles with Goodrich tires, Christy Anatomic saddles, tandem spokes and reinforced forks. They carried a Krag-Jorgensen rifle weighing 10lb, a cartridge belt with 50 rounds, a canteen, blanket, and half a shelter tent, in addition to rations. After reaching St Louis on July 24, 1897, Lt Moss informed the *Army & Navy Journal*: "The trip has proved beyond peradventure my contention that the bicycle has a place in modern warfare. In every kind of weather, over all sorts of roads, we averaged 50 miles a day. At the end of the journey we are all in good physical condition. Seventeen tires and half a dozen frames is the sum of our

damage. The practical result of the trip shows that an Army Bicycle Corps can travel twice as fast as cavalry or infantry under any conditions, and at one third the cost and effort."

CUBA, 1898

The buffalo soldiers' first combat deployment since the end of the Indian Wars followed the outbreak of war between the USA and Spain following an accidental explosion that sank the USS *Maine* in Havana Harbor on February 15, 1898. Cuban guerrillas had been in rebellion against their Spanish overlords since 1895, and the American public had become increasingly alarmed by the inhumane methods used by the Spanish government in trying to quell this revolt. Convinced that his warship had been sabotaged, President William McKinley received permission from Congress on April 19 to use the US Army and Navy to force Spain to renounce its sovereignty over Cuba.

Commanded by MajGen William Shafter, the US force that prepared to invade Cuba consisted of the 5th Corps, and included all four black Regular regiments. The 9th and 10th Cavalry formed part of the Cavalry Division, under ex-Confederate cavalry leader Gen Joseph Wheeler, USV, while the 24th and 25th Infantry served in the 2nd Division. Twelve African-American Volunteer units also filled out the ranks of the US Army during the Spanish-American War. These included four of the ten "Immune Regiments," whose ranks were filled with those supposed to possess immunity from yellow fever, or likely to be exempt from "diseases incident to tropical climates" – a dangerous fiction.

The detachment of the 25th Infantry, commanded by Lt James A.Moss, that tested the use of the bicycle in rugged terrain in 1896. After the end of hostilities in Cuba in 1898 the 25th's 100-strong bicycle company was sent to perform riot duty in Havana. (K.Ross Toole Archives, University of Montana – Missoula)

Armed with M1896 Krag-Jörgensen rifles, the 24th Infantry train in full marching order prior to departure for Cuba in 1898. (LC-USZ62-119314)

The four Regular regiments were ordered to mobilize during March–April 1898. The 9th and 10th Cavalry and 24th Infantry assembled at "Camp Thomas" in Chickamauga Park near Lytle, GA, while elements of the 25th Infantry proceeded to Key West, Florida. This was the first time in their history that the buffalo soldiers had been ordered to the southeastern United States, and the first time that the bulk of the American people even realized that their standing army included regiments composed wholly of black soldiers. On April 30 the *Army & Navy Journal* reported that the "Buffalo soldiers, colored, 25th Inf [were] the admiration of all the colored belles" in Chattanooga as they passed through on their way to Chickamauga Park.

Having served at remote frontier posts for many years, the African-American soldiers, in their turn, were unused to seeing poverty-stricken blacks. Walking down Meeting Street, Chickamauga, Sgt J.P.Smith, 10th Cavalry, spied a 12-year-old black boy dressed in rags, and insisted on taking him into a clothing store where he "bought him a complete outfit, hat, shoes and clothing, for the sum of $10, and made him put them on." However, the black soldiers were not so popular with the whites. Racial tension was nothing new for the southeast, but the sudden arrival of self-confident black soldiers unaccustomed to suffering blatant discrimination created an explosive atmosphere. Soon after they reached that city, an editorial in the Tampa *Morning Tribune* seemed to promise trouble: "The colored infantrymen stationed in Tampa... have made themselves very offensive to the people of the city... The men insist upon being treated as white men are treated."

The African-American regiments were next moved to the staging area near Tampa, where a six weeks' wait in May–June seemed interminable.

The 10th Cavalry, the last to arrive, was located at Lakeland about 22 miles east of Tampa, while the 9th encamped at Port Tampa. The 24th Infantry was situated on the "Heights" outside the city. On June 7 orders were finally received to embark for Cuba. The 24th Infantry sailed on the *City of Washington*, while the 25th boarded the *Concho* with the 4th US Infantry and 2nd Massachusetts Volunteers. Required to leave their horses behind for lack of shipping space, the cavalry regiments discovered that they would be expected to fight as infantry. The 9th Cavalry sailed on the *Miami*, while the 10th was transported on the *Leona*, with the exception of Troops C & F who sailed on the *Alamo*. The contingent from the 10th Cavalry consisted of the 1st Squadron commanded by Maj S.T.Norvell, and composed of Troops A, B, E & I; and the 2nd Squadron, under Maj Theodore J.Wint, consisting of Troops C, D, F & G. To their disappointment, most of the other personnel remained at Lakeland in charge of the horses and baggage.

The exception to the general dismounting of the troopers was a detachment of 50 men from Troops A, H & M commanded by Lt C.P.Johnson, which was assigned to perform a "special mission" in Cuba as mounted troops. Accompanied by the Cuban Gen Munez, 375 assorted Cubans and a large quantity of arms and munitions for Gen Maximo Gomez, these buffalo soldiers sailed from Tampa aboard the *Florida*, under escort from the gunboat *Peoria*, on June 21.

Las Guásimas

Finally sailing from Tampa on June 8, the flotilla of 32 ships carrying nearly 17,000 men of the main expedition made landfall at Siboney on the southeast tip of Cuba on June 22. As soon as they were disembarked, Shafter's brigades began pushing inland along the road from Siboney towards Santiago de Cuba. Overtaking BrigGen Henry W.Lawton's 2nd Inf Div, advanced elements of the dismounted Cavalry Div under MajGen Wheeler fought the first engagement of the campaign on June 24 at Las Guásimas, a junction of two trails about 3 miles inland. Deployed in two columns, eight troops of the 1st US Volunteer Cavalry (the 'Rough Riders'), commanded by Col Leonard Wood, with future president LtCol Theodore Roosevelt as second in command, proceeded along an overgrown jungle trail to the left, while four troops each of the 1st and 10th Cavalry, led by Gen Wheeler, followed two separate routes on their right.

Without a trail to follow, and advancing "as blind men would through the dense underbrush," the buffalo soldiers took time to hack their way through the jungle, and got into battle about 20 minutes after the first US troops engaged the enemy. With orders to fight a rearguard action, the Spanish opened fire with their Krupp mountain gun detachment and smokeless-cartridge Mauser rifles, and held back the American advance for about an hour. Fanning out, the US troopers groped their way forward and eventually flushed the Spaniards out of their positions; the 10th Cavalry, commanded by LtCol T.A.Baldwin, suffered one man killed and eight wounded. In the heat of the moment the absent-minded ex-Confederate Joe Wheeler's reaction to the Spanish withdrawal was to jump up and shout, "Come on, boys, we got the damned Yankees on the run!" Nothing now lay between Shafter's beachhead and the outer defenses of Santiago de Cuba.

El Caney

The key to the capture of the city was the San Juan Heights, which were held by entrenched Spanish troops. On July 1 the attack on these positions was assigned to the 2nd Div, supported by the dismounted Cavalry Division. Meanwhile, as diversions, a brigade commanded by Gen H.Duffield, with Navy support, followed the railroad line down the coast from Siboney towards Santiago; while the 1st Inf Div, including the 25th Infantry, marched north to capture an entrenched Spanish position at El Caney. Both of these detached forces were eventually to march back to the Heights in support of the main attack.

Commanded by Gen Joaquin Vara de Rey, the Spanish defenses at El Caney consisted of a stone fort, four wooden blockhouses, and a stone church that had been loop-holed and garrisoned; these works were interconnected by slit trenches and surrounded by barbed wire. The Spanish positions on San Juan Heights were similar, consisting of several blockhouses linked by trenches to those on neighboring Kettle Hill. According to Gen Shafter's plan, El Caney should have fallen within two hours; but 520 Spanish troops managed to hold back some 6,600 Americans for about eight hours.

According to Spanish Lt José Muller, the defenders "threw forth a hail of projectiles upon the enemy, while one company after another, without any protection, rushed with veritable fury upon the city." The

Reproduced in *McClures Magazine* in September 1898, this gouache painting by William Glackens depicts the 25th and 12th Infantry taking the stone fort of El Viso, near El Caney, on July 1, 1898. The lone figure struggling up the hill in advance of the main body of troops may possibly be journalist James Creelman, who later falsely claimed that he – not the buffalo soldiers – had captured the Spanish flag. (Anne S.K.Brown Military Collection, Brown University Library)

12th Infantry attacked the stone fort from the east, while the 25th, commanded by LtCol Aaron S.Daggett, approached from the southeast. In the aftermath, both regiments claimed to have received the surrender of the Spanish strongpoint. According to a report by Lt James A.Moss published in the *Army and Navy Journal*, Cos D, E, G & H of the 25th Infantry advanced about 600 yards towards the fort "by a series of rushes over exposed ground, crawling up streams, working their way through 'Spanish dagger' [cactus], thick underbrush... during which they were subjected to most galling front and flank fires from several different sources."

Reaching the crest of a small hill about 150 yards from the fort, these men delivered a general fusillade for about 15 minutes, before orders were given for only marksmen and sharpshooters to fire. "For ten minutes or more," continued Moss, "these men poured lead into every door, porthole and rifle pit in sight, the mortar, brick and earth fairly flying! The Spaniards were now panic stricken and demoralized, and with neither hats nor rifles were frantically running from the stone fort to the rifle pits, and from the rifle pits to the stone fort, while our men were shooting them down like sheep."

At this point the buffalo soldiers observed a white flag being waved from the fort, but continued Spanish flanking fire from a nearby blockhouse made it impossible for them to advance any further to accept the surrender. Meanwhile, a company of the 12th Infantry rushed forward, poured into the fort through a large hole created by the US

Entitled "Forgotten Heroes," this painting by Fletcher R.Ransom depicts Troop C, 9th Cavalry, commanded by Capt Taylor, leading the charge up Kettle Hill during the battle for Santiago de Cuba on July 1, 1898. It was published in *Harper's Weekly* on October 15 that year – coincidentally, the same issue carried illustrations of the battle of Omdurman on September 2, including the charge of the 21st Lancers in which Winston Churchill took part.

artillery, and received the white flag. At the same time, Pvts T.C.Butler, Co H, and J.H.Jones, Co D, 25th Infantry, entered the fort and took possession of the Spanish flag. When he presented a piece of this flag to Lt Vernon A.Caldwell, 25th Infantry, Butler informed that officer: "I went off ahead of the company, and when the artillery blew that hole in the wall I went in and got the flag, and along came a white man dressed something like an officer and made me give it to him, but I tore a corner off the flag anyway." This white man was probably James Creelman, war correspondent for the New York *Journal*, who claimed to have been "the first American inside the walls of the fort," and who was shot through the shoulder while "recovering the Spanish flag." The 25th Infantry sustained eight killed and 27 wounded at El Caney, and Pvt Conny Gray, Co D, earned the Certificate of Merit for "fearlessly exposing himself, under a heavy fire, applying a first-aid bandage and carrying his wounded captain a considerable distance to shelter, and then rejoining his company, participating in the action to its close."

San Juan Heights

The main assault on San Juan Heights on July 1 was actually an attack on several different defended hilltops. General Sumner's dismounted Cavalry Div – composed of the 1st, 3rd, 6th, 9th and 10th Regular regiments, plus the 1st US Volunteer Cavalry – went up that part of the range north of the sunken road, known as Little San Juan Hill or Kettle Hill. The 1st Bde, 1st Div, under Gen Hawkins – the 6th and 16th Infantry – assaulted the main section of the Heights afterwards named "Blockhouse Hill." The 3rd Bde, 1st Div, commanded by Col Wickoff (but led by LtCol E.P.Ewers after Wickoff was killed) – the 9th, 13th and

Photographed at Camp Forse, Huntsville, Alabama, on the occasion of his retirement on November 1, 1898, Sgt George Berry of Troop D, 10th Cavalry, holds in his right hand the bullet-riddled regimental flag he carried up Kettle Hill in Cuba on July 1 (see Plate A). The other is the national color of the 10th Cavalry, though oddly retouched in this photograph. (Fort Huachuca Museum)

Troopers of the 9th Cavalry man a sand-bagged breastwork in Cuba, July 1898. They wear drab campaign hats, dark blue 1883-pattern flannel overshirts, and sky-blue kersey trousers. (Anne S.K.Brown Military Collection, Brown University Library)

24th Infantry – attacked that part of the Heights south of the Santiago road. The 10th, 2nd and 21st Infantry of Col Pearson's 2nd Bde scaled San Juan Hill immediately to the south of Hawkins' brigade.

While waiting for orders to attack, the buffalo soldiers came under heavy fire when an observation balloon of the US Signal Corps was towed down the road and hovered above them. At this point the men were ordered to slip off their blanket rolls and haversacks, which were left under guard. The first line, consisting of four troops of the 9th Cavalry under Col John M.Hamilton, took cover in the sunken road. When the Rough Riders caught up with them LtCol Roosevelt, still mounted on his charger "Little Texas," informed a captain in command of the black troopers that they "would not take these hills by firing at them," and that the position must be rushed. The captain replied that he could not do so without orders and did not know the whereabouts of his commander. "Then I am the ranking officer here," Roosevelt replied, "and I give the order to charge!" When the Regular still hesitated to follow orders from a Volunteer officer, Roosevelt said, "Then let my men through, sir." With that, the Rough Riders began to pass through the Regulars, many of whom jumped up and joined in the advance.

Corporal John R.Conn, who was farther along the line with Co H, 24th Infantry, recalled: "The orders from our colonel were: 'Twenty fourth Infantry, move forward 150 yards and lie down.' With a last look at our arms and ammunition – yes and a little prayer – we started, and such a volley as they sent into us! It was then that Sgt [D.T.] Brown was shot almost at the river bank. We had to cut and destroy a barbed wire fence… someone sounded 'Let us charge' on the bugle. When that pack of demons swept forward the Spaniards stood as long as mortals could stand, then quit their trenches and retired to the trenches around Santiago."

The cavalrymen had the shortest distance to cover once they had crossed the San Juan river and reached the foot of the Heights. As the black troopers waded the river the 10th Cavalry's Regimental Sergeant Major, Edward L.Baker, Jr, left the cover of the bank to save a wounded comrade from drowning, for which he was later awarded the Medal of Honor. The 9th and 10th Cavalry went up Kettle Hill with the Rough Riders to their right. Troops A, B, E & I of the 10th, under Maj Norvell, formed the first line, followed by Troops C, F & G led by Maj Wint. Having crossed the river farther down, Troop D of the 10th attached itself to Hawkins' infantry brigade and joined in the assault on

"Blockhouse Hill." Corporals John Walker and Luchious Smith were at "the head and front of the assault," and both were later awarded the Certificate of Merit; the latter award was subsequently replaced by the Distinguished Service Medal.

Elsewhere along the line, other elements of the cavalry also began to stumble up the steep 120ft hill. Irregularities in the 30-degree slopes partially masked the defenders' view; grabbing tufts of grass, the US troopers scrambled upwards, with men of different units becoming intermingled. According to the *Army and Navy Journal*, several musicians of the 6th and 10th Cavalry lifted their bugles as they climbed and "blew the 'Star Spangled Banner' into the Spanish lines."

Major Wint and adjutant 1st Lt Marvin Hill Barnum, 10th Cavalry, were both wounded, and Lt W.E.Smith of Troop G was killed. Lieutenant Frank R.McCoy, Troop A, was severely wounded at the height of the action, and was commended for gallantry; Lt Richard L.Livermore of the same troop was commended for bravery for capturing the blockhouse where he was wounded. Three Spanish bullets struck Capt John Bigelow, Jr, commanding Troop D, when he was only 75 yards from the blockhouse. Lieutenants H.O.Willard, Troop B, and H.C.Whitehead, Troop F, were also wounded. Corporal John E.Lewis of the 10th's Troop H recalled that "About every troop… lost its officers… and non-commissioned officers took their places and led the troops on to a victory."

In the first line of that regiment, Farrier Sherman Harris, Troop I, kept in advance and picked out the best cover for the men in his immediate rear. Sergeant Thomas Griffith, Troop C, cut the barbed wire so the buffalo soldiers and Rough Riders could scramble through. Wagoner John Boland and Pvt Elise Jones also showed extreme courage during the advance. When Lt T.A.Roberts, commanding Troop G in the second line, fell wounded, Trumpeter James H.Cooper and Pvt William J.Davis assisted him back to a dressing station under heavy Spanish fire.

Men of the 9th Cavalry in quarantine at Camp Wikoff on Montauk Point, Long Island, after their return from the Cuban campaign. The trooper with the bandana standing second from right is Augustus Walley, one of four enlisted men in the regiment to eventually be awarded a retrospective Silver Star for bravery at San Juan Heights in July 1898. (USAMHI)

Nearby, as he advanced with his men of the 3rd Cavalry, Color Sgt J.E.Andrews took a bullet in the stomach. Calling in vain for a lieutenant to take the colors, he stumbled back down the hill, still clutching the flag. Following behind with Troop G, 10th Cavalry, Color Sgt George Berry snatched it up and carried both regiments' colors to the top of the ridge. When questioned by *Harper's Weekly* in November 1898, Berry replied: "Where did my courage come from? It came from our 'war chief,' Captain [Charles G.] Ayres [Troop E]. When I saw him leading his men, waving his hat in the air, shouting out like a trumpet to the soldiers to follow, I took the two sets of colors and ran, calling as I ran: 'Dress on the colors, boys! Dress on the colors!'"

Meanwhile, on the main Heights men of the 24th Infantry under Capt Arthur C.Ducat and Lt Henry G.Lyon scrambled towards a blockhouse defended by 35 Spaniards, but both officers and a number of men fell wounded before they reached the crest. Unable to break through the heavy wooden doors and planked-up windows, 19 men climbed on to the red tile roof to drop through a hole left by a shell. Four were killed at once; the remaining 15 captured the building after a few minutes of hand-to-hand fighting.

The 9th Cavalry had reached the crest of Kettle Hill, led by Capt Eugene D.Dimmick; now the troopers struggled over a wire fence and began to advance across the valley towards the second Spanish line. The Spaniards retreated long before the cavalrymen reached their trenches, and by 1.50pm the Americans had secured the entire length of the San Juan Heights. However, the Spanish artillery continued to shell them. Assigned with a detail of two men to temporary duty with the Gatling gun detachment under Lt John H.Parker, 13th Infantry, Sgt John Graham of the 9th's Troop E showed great courage towards the end of the day while saving that officer's life. In his recommendation for the Medal of Honor, Lt Parker stated that Graham "rendered particularly valuable service in keeping the ammunition supply up at this time, and at one time, when a shell was about to explode in the battery, endeavored to shield his commanding officer, myself, with his own body. His services at this time, in keeping the ammunition going, were particularly dangerous as it had to be carried some distance exposed to the view and fire of the enemy, but he so well performed this work that the Gatlings were enabled to drive the enemy's gunners away from their guns by directing a steady and continuous fire upon their pieces."

After the battle, 1st Sgt Adam Houston, Troop C, 10th Cavalry, recalled: "We had been on the hill about three hours and my gun was almost red hot. I had fired about 175 rounds of ammunition, and being very thirsty, I gladly accepted the [water] detail, as the hill was ours then and we had been shooting at nothing for about an hour. What a sight was presented as I re-crossed the flat in front of San Juan. The dead and wounded soldiers! It was indescribable. One would have to see it to know what it was like, and having once seen it, I truly hope I may never see it again."

Casualties and recognition

In fact, 26 buffalo soldiers lay dead on the field, among several times that many wounded. The 24th Infantry suffered some of the heaviest casualties in the infantry assault on the main ridge, having two officers –

including the CO, LtCol E.H.Liscum – and 11 men killed, and six officers and 71 men wounded. Colonel Hamilton was shot dead leading the 9th Cavalry up Kettle Hill; seven enlisted men were also killed, and LtCol Henry Carroll was wounded. Of 450 men of the 10th Cavalry, seven were killed, 72 were wounded, and four were listed as missing.

Shamefully, most of the battlefield accounts published in the weeks after the action ignored the deeds of the black troops in Cuba, and generally cast them in a supporting role. However, a report in the *Army and Navy Journal* dated September 2, 1898, indicates that the 1st US Volunteer Cavalry had found themselves in need of support after being pinned down by heavy fire: "The Rough Riders were in a bad position on San Juan Hill at one time, and it is generally admitted they could not have held their position but for the splendid charge of the Ninth Cavalry to their support. After the worst of the fighting was over a Rough Rider, finding himself near one of the colored troopers, walked up and grasped his hand, saying 'We've got you fellows to thank for getting us out of a bad hole.'" Frank Knox, another member of the 1st USVC, added, "I never saw braver men anywhere."

Sergeant Graham of the 9th Cavalry's Troop E received his Medal of Honor for saving the life of Lt Parker, and the Certificate of Merit was awarded to 29 other buffalo soldiers for the various actions in Cuba –

one-seventh of the total awarded for the war. The CM was awarded to nine men of the 24th Infantry, plus one man in the 25th at El Caney. Seven CMs went to men of the 9th Cavalry and 12 to the 10th; two of these recipients were subsequently selected for commissions in the black regiments of US Volunteer Infantry organized for later service in Cuba – 1st Sgt Peter McCowan of the 10th Cavalry became a second lieutenant in the 7th USVI, and Sgt Elisha Jackson of the 9th a second lieutenant in the 10th US Volunteer Infantry. McCowan would also serve later as a first lieutenant in the 48th USVI, a black regiment raised for service in the Philippines.

After World War I the War Department began a systematic review of official reports and records of military service, and eight other black soldiers were retrospectively awarded the newly instituted Silver Star medal (third only to the Medal of Honor and Distinguished Service Cross) for bravery during the Spanish-American War. These were Presly Holliday, Isaac Bailey, John Buck and Augustus Walley, 10th Cavalry; and George Driscoll, Robert L.Duvall, Elbert Wolley and Richard Curtis, 24th Infantry.

Rescue at Tayabacoa

While most black Regulars were fighting on foot at El Caney and Santiago de Cuba, we must recall that Lt Carter P.Johnson's 50-strong mounted detachment from Troops A, H & M, 10th Cavalry, had been detailed to perform a "special mission" – the delivery of much needed supplies to the Cuban rebels. Accompanying Gen Munez and his 375 soldiers, 65 mules and packs, rations, clothing and ammunition, they sailed on the steamship *Florida*, accompanied by the steamship *Fanita* and escorted by the gunboat *Peoria*, on June 21. Arriving off the south coast of Cuba eight days later, they attempted a landing at the San Juan river, but found this impossible due to a long coral reef. Sailing down the coast towards Tunas, a landing party consisting of 28 Americans and several Cubans rowed ashore at Tayabacoa to reconnoiter the enemy fortifications. They hid their boats in the heavy jungle and began creeping inland; but they stumbled into view of a Spanish blockhouse, and came under heavy fire. As they fell back towards the shore several Americans fell wounded, and five or six Cubans were killed. When they reached the water they found their boats destroyed by enemy artillery, and were overrun by the Spanish.

Aboard the *Florida*, a detachment of Cubans was hastily organized to go ashore and rescue the captured soldiers. Four separate attempts were met with heavy fire, and the Cubans were forced to return to the ships. As darkness fell, Lt George Ahearn, 25th Infantry, who had accompanied the expedition, agreed to lead one more rescue attempt. Going below, he asked for volunteers to make a fifth effort under cover of darkness; without hesitation, Pvts George Wanton, Fitz Lee, Dennis Bell and William H.Thompkins stepped forward. The five men rowed ashore, and as they secured their boat the Spaniards opened a heavy but blind fire. Ignoring the Mauser rounds cracking over their heads, the five volunteers slowly worked their way through the thick undergrowth. Eventually the Spanish ceased fire, and in the eerie silence Pvt Thompkins heard a quiet plea for help; following the sound, he found the missing men locked in a stockade.

As he smashed the gate the Spanish opened fire once more. Two o the buffalo soldiers provided covering fire while the rescued prisoner were helped to the boat; all 16 surviving members of the advance party were recovered, and although the enemy continued firing, by 3am L Ahearn's volunteers and the rescued shore party were safely aboard the *Florida*. Lieutenant Johnson refused Pvt Wanton's offer to return to retrieve the bodies of their dead comrades.

Their problems were not over, however; for while attempting to ge closer to the shoreline during the prolonged rescue mission, the *Florida* had run aground. For 24 hours she was at the mercy of Spanish batteries, since the gunboat *Peoria* was too small to haul the large transport off despite efforts to lighten her. However, at about noon the next day the larger gunboat *Helena* (Cdr W.T.Swinburne) unexpectedly hove into view, shelled the blockhouse, and successfully refloated the *Florida*. At Lt Johnson's request, the commanders of the *Peoria* and *Helena* continued to lay down a concentrated fire on the Spanish positions while the *Florida* and *Fanita* quietly steamed 40 miles down the coast to Palo Alto, where they successfully landed their men, horses and supplies. The buffalo soldiers joined forces with Gen Gomez and fough the remainder of the campaign under his command, finally rejoining their regiment at Montauk in September 1898. For their conspicuou gallantry during the rescue at Tayabacoa, all four black trooper received the Medal of Honor on June 23, 1899.

Company L in Puerto Rico

With the Spanish capitulation in Cuba on July 16, US forces turned their attention to Puerto Rico, the one remaining Spanish possession in the Caribbean. In charge of the operation was Gen Nelson Miles commanding the First Army Corps. American forces landed on July 2 and, in a 19-day campaign with very few US casualties, subjugated the Spanish garrison under CaptGen Manuel Macas y Casado. A unit of the landing force was the 6th Massachusetts Volunteer Infantry commanded by Col Charles F.Woodward – in whose ranks were the only African-American Volunteers to see combat during the war. Raised in Boston, MA, and mobilized under the first call for volunteers on April 23, 1898, Co L of the 6th Massachusetts was commanded by black officers Capt William J.Williams, 1st Lt William H.Jackson and 2nd L George W.Braxton. It was also the only black unit to be attached to an otherwise white regiment. According to *Leslie's Illustrated Newspaper* of June 23, 1898, Co L was the best behaved and most thoroughly equipped company to be sent from Massachusetts; the piece concluded "Every one of these colored troops is a marksman."

Part of the Provisional Division under BrigGen Guy V.Henry (the former regimental commander of the 10th Cavalry), the 6th Massachusetts landed at Guánica on the south coast of Puerto Rico or July 25. Although they faced only slight opposition Gen Henry took nothing for granted, and ordered BrigGen Henry Garretson to assemble seven companies (A, C, E, G, K, L & M) of the 6th Massachusetts, plus one company of the 6th Illinois, for a move on the railroad terminus a Yauco, five miles north of Guánica. Its capture would help secure the port of Ponce – a deeper harbor than Guánica – for three more invasion flotillas which were expected to arrive soon.

Approaching Yauco, Garretson ordered the Illinois company to occupy part of the Seboruco Hills on his right, overlooking a nearby hacienda thought to be occupied by Spanish troops. The Illinois men dug in and sent scouts toward the hacienda, and shortly afterwards Cos L & M of the 6th Massachusetts arrived as reinforcements. Meanwhile, some Spanish infantry dug in on another nearby hilltop detected the movement and opened fire at about 2.00am on July 26. Garretson immediately committed the remaining five Massachusetts companies to an attack; they swept the Spanish before them, suffering four wounded, including Cpl W.S.Carpenter and Pvt B.Bostic of Company L.

About a week later Gen Miles held an investigation into the conduct of the 6th Massachusetts during the first two days of the campaign – lack of discipline on a hard march from Guánica to Ponce had been reported to Gen Garretson (who was prejudiced against black troops, despite the reported high standards of Company L). Miles requested the resignation of Col Woodward and replaced him with Col Frank Rice, a Regular officer.

Return to the United States

During the remaining operations in Cuba the 24th Infantry remained on San Juan Heights until July 10, when it was moved half a mile, though still in an important position on the exposed left flank. Yellow fever soon broke out in the camps and, in line with the stereotypical view that blacks were physically better able to deal with tropical conditions, this regiment was ordered to the yellow fever camp at Siboney to serve as nurses and hospital orderlies. A report in the *Army & Navy Journal* of February 4, 1899, eventually commended the 24th Infantry for this service, stating that "its fearless attendance of the sick elicited the highest praises, and undoubtedly contributed materially to the excellent results of the medical service." A later reference to this service in the same journal stated that the "colored soldiers died daily at this post of duty." Sailing from Cuba on August 27, 1898, the 24th Infantry had been "reduced by bullets and yellow fever to fewer than 400 men," and received "an ovation on the wharf prior to its departure."

On their return to the US the buffalo soldiers joined their white comrades at Montauk Point on Long Island, New York, where they spent six weeks in quarantine to prevent the spread of diseases picked up in Cuba, such as malaria, typhoid, dysentery and, in some cases, yellow fever. By the end of September the 9th Cavalry had taken up station at Fort Grant, Arizona. After a short spell at Huntsville, AL, the 10th Cavalry was back in Texas by January 29, 1899, although they returned to Cuba for a further tour of duty in 1900. The 24th Infantry arrived back at Fort Douglas, UT, on October 1, 1898. On their return from Cuba the 25th Infantry established their new headquarters at Fort Logan, CO, while other companies of the regiment were stationed in Arizona and New Mexico.

THE PHILIPPINES, 1899–1902

Following the Treaty of Paris of December 10, 1898, which ended the Spanish-American War and ceded Guam, the Philippine Islands and Puerto Rico to the US, hostilities broke out between American forces and Filipino insurgents under Emilio Aguinaldo on February 4, 1899. A Filipino force of about 20,000 attacked Manila, and the US garrison of about 11,000 fought fiercely to prevent being pushed into the sea. After much hard fighting the Americans were able to throw the insurgents back, and Gen Arthur MacArthur (father of Douglas) followed up with a counter-attack that ended in the occupation of Caloocan, north of Manila. The campaign then ground to a halt due to insufficient US troop strength – Army regulations required that Volunteers, who made up 75 percent of the available force, be sent home because the war with Spain was over. Hence, Gen Ewell S. Otis (nicknamed "Colonel Blimp"), commander of US forces in the Philippines, was compelled to stay on the defensive until the arrival of reinforcements.

Meanwhile, Congress authorized the organization of 25 new regiments of two-year Volunteer infantry, the last two of which were the black 48th and 49th USVI, authorized via the Act of March 2, 1899. The black Regulars also saw service in the Philippines: towards the end of

June 1899 elements of the 24th and 25th Infantry were en route for Manila. Major J.M.Thompson and four companies of the 24th sailed from San Francisco aboard the *Zealandia* on June 22, 1899, arriving on July 24; two companies of the 25th sailed from the same port aboard the *Valencia* six days later, and further companies from both regiments followed shortly thereafter.

Campaigning in Luzon

Within three days of arrival in the Philippines the black Regular infantry were in the Manila defenses, and helping to man four miles of trenches running from Caloocan to Block House No.5 on the Caloocan–La Loma line. After the rainy season passed both units took part in MacArthur's offensive against the insurgent strongholds in Pampanga and Tarlac provinces of central Luzon. Marching towards the volcanic Mt Arayat, and reaching the town of Arayat on October 6, the 24th Infantry met the enemy and had a "hard fight." During this action 1st Sgt Jacob W.Stevens and Sgt Tennie Cranshaw, Co K, both earned the CM for commanding their men with "coolness and good judgment" during an insurgent attack near Santa Ana.

On October 9, the day that the 25th Infantry was ordered to march from the Caloocan–La Loma line for Bamban north of Mt Arayat, the insurgents made a demonstration against positions still held by that regiment. Private C.W.Cordin, Co B, recalled: "As I was on outpost at the time, about a half mile from the company, doing picket duty... we noticed a file of queer looking people coming out of the bamboo woods, and as

21

These NCOs of the 25th Infantry were photographed at Bamban, Luzon, in 1899. Sergeant William Chambers, Co M (left), and Commissary Sgt D.P.Green (right), in drab campaign hats, dark blue shirts, and khaki trousers and leggings, stand either side of SgtMaj A.A.Morrow, who wears a khaki blouse with what appear to be brown canvas fatigue trousers. (*Buffalo Soldier Regiment*)

about 200 Chinese coolies had been carrying bamboo from these woods to our lines, to build our supply road, we did not pay much attention to them as they were dressed just as the Chinese coolies are. All at once they threw out their skirmish line. As the body of men did this another body to their left marched out of the woods as skirmishers, and before we could send word to the company, the insurgents opened the battle, and it seemed as if every bullet came towards us two lonely men. In a moment's notice we were down in our trenches that are near our picket tent. We must work, and this is where our target practice came into good play. We worked like demons... for about an hour we kept them from advancing. At the end of that time Company B came out to our outpost on the left, volley firing. This made the Filipinos sick and they soon scampered to the woods. We lost ten men killed and one wounded."

While stationed at Bamban and Mabalacat, the 25th Infantry received intelligence from Filipino deserters that O'Donnell, about six miles northwest of Bamban, was filled with insurgent soldiers and weapons. Guided by one of the deserters, about 400 picked men from Cos B, E & K under Capt Harry A.Leonhauser set out for that place on the night of November 18, taking a roundabout route through the foothills for the sake of surprise. At about 4am the next morning they encountered a palm-leaf shack and spied men moving inside. A detail of Co K under Lt Bates silently surrounded the outpost and demanded its surrender, which was accepted. As the occupants passed rifles and ammunition out of the window the barking of the village dogs gave the alarm, and the black troops rushed on to complete their mission.

In the *Denver Times* later that month an officer who took part stated that: "There was an immediate move toward the town, and a few scattered shots were fired as our troops entered. We were in the town now and the colored soldiers showed a grim and great earnestness in their work of gathering in prisoners, rifles and bolos (long-bladed knives). Strong black arms caught fleeing insurgents upon the streets and hauled them from under beds and beneath houses. Native women screamed in alarm and on their knees offered money and food to the American troops." At 6am the command regrouped, bringing in as prisoners the entire Filipino garrison consisting of seven officers and 200 men. They used bull carts from the village to carry away about 225 rifles and nearly 10,000 rounds of ammunition.

While posted in northern Luzon the black Regulars spent much of their time on long scouting expeditions and patrols. On December 7, 1899, Cpl John H.Johnson, Co F, 24th Infantry, and Pvts Earnest Stokes, Lig J.Clark, Benjamin H.Goode and Amos Stuckey of Co H, earned the CM for "most distinguished gallantry in action" during a scout near Naguilian on the west coast of the island.

On January 5, 1900, Cos B, K & M, 25th Infantry, again under the command of Capt Leonhauser, left their camp at Magalang and attacked the insurgent stronghold of Gen Aquino at Camansi near Mt Arayat. According to the report on this operation, "The troops scaled heights of great difficulty, and crawled through dense undergrowth. Lieutenant William T.Schenck, 25th Infantry, particularly distinguished himself in leading the advance, as did also Lieutenant A.C.Martin, and the enemy was driven off with what was believed to be considerable loss." Sergeant James R.Lightfoot, Co K, received the CM for "distinguished gallantry displayed in the advance upon a concealed enemy" during this action. The insurgent barracks were destroyed with large quantities of stores; American losses amounted to only one man killed – Cpl M.Washington of Company B.

According to Lt Schenck, the insurgents "evidently had all they wanted of the '*soldados negros*'. After we had gotten the wounded dressed we started back and I covered the retreat with the scouts." The battle report concluded, "Five American prisoners fell into our hands [i.e. were rescued], but not until they had been shot and so brutally boloed that but two recovered."

On January 6–7, 1900, a force of about 1,000 insurgents attacked the village of Iba on the west coast, which was occupied by Co F, 25th Infantry commanded by Capt Joseph P.O'Neil. The buffalo soldiers held their ground in three "defensible buildings" including a church. At the signal of a lighted candle in the church window, O'Neil ordered his men to sally forth and form up with "bayonets charged." According to the report of Col Burt, the officer "ordered the trumpeter to sound the 'Charge' and his men raised a yell and with Captain O'Neil at the head they went at the enemy and cleaned them out in a handsome manner."

On July 4, 1900, a 40-strong scouting party of the 24th Infantry encountered a large group of insurgents near Manacling. According to the *Army & Navy Journal*, "The rebels had the little body of colored troops 'horse-shoed,' but they fought their way out with little loss to their party and much damage to the insurgents. The American colored men fought like demons and soon had their antagonists on a sprint in all directions.

The insurgents left 16 killed and 30 wounded on the field. Lieutenant Mitchell was seriously wounded, and one enlisted man was killed and two wounded. Lieutenant Mitchell and the men were highly praised for their tact and bravery." On August 11, 1900, elements of the 24th Infantry captured 165 insurgents, led by Roberto Grassa, who probably belonged to the band that had attacked them the previous month.

Meanwhile, by March 1900 the black 49th USVI, commanded by Col William H.Back, saw action at the northern end of Luzon. Four companies of that regiment left Manila on the transport *Aztec* and landed at St Vincent, from whence they marched overland to Aparri where they established their regimental headquarters and were soon joined by four more companies. On March 20, a patrol of 30 black Volunteers from this regiment encountered a band of insurgents and killed two, capturing arms and ammunition. During another patrol, Lt Gilmer of the 49th began to suspect that the Filipino guide who claimed to know the location of a band of "*insurrectos*" was leading them into an ambush. Halting his men in a bamboo thicket, he ordered the guide to exchange clothing with one of the buffalo soldiers, and gave him a rifle and ammunition belt. The party proceeded and came to a river, which the guide insisted had to be crossed in order to attack the insurgents. As the guide was forced out into the water at gunpoint, shots rang out from the opposite bank and the insurgents revealed their position. The black Volunteers then flanked the enemy, and after "a hot fight, won the day, capturing rifles and ammunition."

A group photograph of Troop F, 10th Cavalry, commanded by Capt P.E.Trippe, taken possibly at Calbayog in Samar during their first tour of duty in the Philippines. The group shows a mixture of old issue 1898-pattern and 1902-pattern service uniforms – typical of the supply system of the day – with 1902-pattern hats. One of the officers wears the blue 1895-pattern cap and undress coat. (USAMHI – B.O.Davis Collection)

Later service

Between October 1900 and June 1901, about 1,000 further clashes occurred between US forces and Filipino insurgents; but after the capture of Emilio Aguinaldo in March 1901 these encounters decreased. However, US forces remained in occupation of the Philippines, and elements of all four black Regular regiments completed further service there between 1901 and 1918. Eight troops of the 9th Cavalry were in the Philippines by September 1900, and Sgt Richard Miller, Co F, was subsequently awarded the CM for "distinguished conduct" when attacked by "several bolomen" near Tagbac on December 17 of that year. A squadron of the 10th Cavalry served in Samar and Panay from May 1901 until June 1902; and the entire regiment returned in 1907 to undertake a two-year tour of duty. The 9th was back in the islands in 1902, taking part in expeditions against the Moros, a fierce Mohammedan people of Mindanao and the Sulu Archipelago, who had never been completely subjugated by the Spanish. The 24th Infantry returned to the Philippines in 1906; on July 24 of that year Sgt John W.Ash and Cpl Preston Askew, Co E, earned the CM for "conspicuous gallantry in action" near Tabon-Tabon in the jungles of Samar, against Pulajanes – followers of Papa Faustino, who claimed to possess messianic powers. The 25th Infantry began their second tour in the Philippines on September 13, 1906, and served against hostile Moros on Mindanao until 1909. A further six buffalo soldiers were awarded Certificates of Merit for life-saving actions in non-combat situations in the Philippines between 1899 and 1914.

THE MEXICAN BORDER, 1914–17

Following the Mexican Revolution of 1910, in 1911 fighting erupted between the "constitutionalist" army of Venustiano Carranza and the rebel forces of Francisco "Pancho" Villa. By late 1915 Villa hoped for American support to obtain the presidency of Mexico, but instead the US government recognized the Carranza regime. An irate Villa swore vengeance, and began attacking Americans in hopes of provoking President Woodrow Wilson's intervention in Mexico. Villa believed that this would discredit the Carranza government with the people of Mexico, and reaffirm his own popularity.

The 10th Cavalry sailed from the Philippines to the USA on May 14, 1909, and arrived in New York harbor on July 25. On July 27 it moved to Fort Ethan Allen, VT, where it remained (apart from a spell at the Cavalry Camp of Instruction at Winchester, VA) until December 8, 1913, when it was ordered back to Fort Huachuca near Tombstone, Arizona. Arriving at its old garrison, the regiment promptly found itself back on duty on the Mexican border which, according to regimental historian Maj E.L.N.Glass, was in "a more than usual turmoil."

Naco, 1914

Both the 9th and 10th Cavalry were ordered to protect American lives and property when fighting occurred between the rival Mexican armies outside Naco, a small town which straddled the border between the US and Mexico, during October 1914. Colonel William C.Brown, leading

A detachment of the 10th Cavalry search for Pancho Villa during the Punitive Expedition of 1916. The mount second from left can be seen to wear the first-pattern M1904 McClellan saddles used during this campaign. (Fort Huachuca Museum)

four troops of the 10th, arrived on the scene during the night of October 7. He was joined by six troops and the machine gun platoon from the 9th Cavalry, under Col John Francis Guilfoyle, who took overall command. Brown deployed west of that part of Naco which lay on the American side of the border, while Guilfoyle occupied the eastern sector. By December 1914 this force had been increased to seven troops from each regiment, plus a machine gun company, for a total of 1,050 men.

During this highly confusing campaign it was difficult for the US soldiers to distinguish between the entrenched pro-Villa rebels (who included Yaqui Indians) under Gen Maytorena, and the Mexican Federal forces commanded by Gen Benjamin Hill. However, they maintained a neutral stance while observing the fighting from their own trenches and rifle pits, with "machine guns all set in action." To make matters worse, American civilians crowded into Naco to watch the fighting. According to Maj Glass, the African-American troopers had "great difficulty… in holding back the crowds of visitors from Bisbee and Douglas who flocked to see the 'battles', in automobiles, wagons and [on] horseback."

The fighting at Naco continued until January 1915, with Mexican bullets ripping through the frame buildings and military tents in and around town on a regular basis. Seven members of the 10th Cavalry were wounded by stray bullets during the performance of this duty, while the 9th sustained one dead and two wounded. Indeed, as the officers of the 10th enjoyed their Thanksgiving meal in a tent about 800 yards from the US Army trenches, their menu contained the caution "Guests will please be careful in dodging stray bullets not to upset the soup." On April 7, 1915, the buffalo soldiers were commended for their "splendid conduct and efficient service" at Naco by Secretary of War Lindley M.Garrison.

The regiments remained on border patrol duty during the remainder of 1915, and continued to encounter hostility from Mexican troops and guerrillas. At Lochiel, AZ, on August 22, a detachment of government soldiers crossed the border and attempted to rustle cattle, but was thwarted by patrols of Troop K, 10th Cavalry. On November 3–4, four troops of the 10th, under Col Brown, protected the citizens of Douglas,

Maj Charles Young as commander of 2nd Sqn, 10th Cavalry during the Punitive Expedition. It was he who led the charge at Aguas Calientes which scattered 150 *Villistas* led by the guerrilla chief Benlan in April 1916, and that summer he was promoted lieutenant-colonel and appointed regimental commander. He wears a pullover 1916-pattern olive drab cotton shirt and 1912-pattern breeches with civilian boots. In June 1917, Young was promoted colonel, but was then retired – allegedly on medical grounds, which he promptly proved false by riding on horseback from his Ohio home to Washington, DC. The racial prejudice of the day would not tolerate a black general in France – the command for which Young was obviously qualified. Cynically restored to active duty in November 1918, he died in Liberia in 1922. (US National Archives)

AZ, during fighting between the rival factions at Agua Prieta, Mexico. On November 21 two enlisted men of Troop F, at an observation post near Monument 117, exchanged fire with Mexicans, and Pvt Willie Norman was wounded. The next day five armed Mexicans rode into a camp at the Santa Cruz river and fired on another detachment of Troop F, who replied with revolver fire. On November 25, Mexican troops crossed the border again and attacked an outpost manned by members of the same troop near Mascarena's Ranch. On the same day, elements of this troop occupied the western outskirts of the border town of Nogales, AZ, which was under attack from both Mexican factions.

The Machine Gun Troop, 10th Cavalry, provided valuable covering fire for the charge at Aguas Calientes on April 1. The pack saddle invented by their CO, Captain Albert E.Phillips, can be seen on the mule at left center. (Fort Huachuca Museum)

PUNITIVE EXPEDITION, 1916

On March 9, 1916, the confrontation reached a new level when Mexican guerrillas led by Pancho Villa raided Columbus, NM; 19 Americans were killed, including seven troopers of the 13th Cavalry. The following day the Southern Department commander, MajGen Frederick Funston, ordered the 10th Cavalry veteran BrigGen John J.Pershing, commander of the 8th Cav Bde, to apprehend the perpetrators and bring back "Villa, dead or alive." For his mission into Chihuahua – which at first had the grudging acquiescence of the ineffective Mexican government – Pershing organized a provisional division designated as the Punitive Expedition, US Army. Designed to pursue bandits in hostile and barren northern Mexico while protecting its lines of communication with infantry, this division differed considerably from the organizations outlined in the *Field Service Regulations*. It consisted of two provisional cavalry brigades, each made up of two cavalry regiments and a field artillery battery, and one infantry brigade of two regiments. Also included were two engineer companies, plus medical, signal, transport, and air units as divisional troops.

Aguas Calientas

The 2nd Cav Bde, under Col George A.Dodd and consisting of the 7th and 10th Cavalry and Bty B, 6th Field Artillery, rendezvoused at Culberson's Ranch, NM, on March 16, 1916. There they were joined by the Machine Gun Troop of the 10th Cavalry, commanded by Capt Albert E.Phillips. Meanwhile, the 24th Infantry, about 1,800 strong, left Columbus on March 28 for service in Mexico guarding the steadily lengthening lines of communication of the mounted troops.

Although cut off from the main column by a heavy snow storm on April 1, the advance guard of Dodd's column surprised a 150-strong party of Villistas by riding 55 miles in 17 hours to attack their encampment at Aguas Calientes, near Parral, about 300 miles inside

Mexico. Under cover of the overhead fire of the machine guns, Troops F and H of the 2nd Sqn, under Maj Charles Young, charged an adobe hut held by the guerrillas. As they increased their speed to a gallop, withholding their fire, the buffalo soldiers began to yell – and the Mexicans ran off into the brush. Three Villistas were killed, and 40 of their horses were captured; the black troopers sustained no casualties, but several of their mounts were killed. During the next few days the 10th Cavalry followed the trail, but the Villistas broke up into smaller groups when they left the mountains, and disappeared once again.

Santa Cruz de Villegas

By April 1916 the Carranza regime was growing hostile to the American military presence, and Mexican government troops began to attack Pershing's units. On April 12, Maj Young's squadron of the 10th rode to the aid of two troops of the 13th Cavalry and one company of the 6th Infantry, under Maj Frank Tompkins, which had come under fire from government troops and an angry mob at Parral, the home town of Pancho Villa. Tompkins' command was forced to retire about eight miles towards Santa Cruz de Villegas, where he made a stand. According to the report of Col Brown: "The village of Santa Cruz was entered quietly and prepared for defense. The roofs of the buildings were manned by riflemen and the enemy kept at 1,200 yards range. At 7.55[pm] I arrived with Major Young's Squadron, and the Machine Gun Troop, Tenth Cavalry, and assumed command. The enemy was still on the hill to the south when we arrived, as was shown by the sounding of their bugles after ours had been sounded."

The mule-mounted "pack platoon" stand in the background while a section of the MG Troop, 10th Cavalry, operate their M1909 Benet-Mercié machine rifle. This French design, rechambered for the US .30-06 cartridge, featured a feed mechanism which avoided the Maxim patent on flexible webbing belts by using long metal stripper clips like the Hotchkiss machine guns; the strips were prone to jamming if not properly handled. (US National Archives)

1st Lt Henry R.Adair, Troop C, 10th Cavalry, killed at Carrizal on June 21, 1916. He wears a 1902-pattern blouse with the prominent "choked-bellows" pockets, and 1902-pattern campaign hat. On both collar sides he displays the cut-out "U.S." in front of the regimental and branch-of-service "9" and "crossed sabers" insignia. *(The History of the Tenth Cavalry, 1866–1921)*

A member of the relief column, Capt George B.Rodney, Troop G, 10th Cavalry, recalled that the "sound of our hoof beats brought Tompkins to the gates and he gave us a warm welcome. He had been wounded in the arm and he had injured a leg by falling over some hasty entrenchments that he had been supervising, and he was glad to see us. As we splashed through the ford he shouted to us. I can hear his words yet. Major Charles Young, one of the six Negro officers of the Army and our Squadron Commander, was riding by me at the head of the advance guard when Tompkins sighted him and called out, 'By God! They were glad to see the Tenth Cavalry at Santiago in '98, but I'm a damn sight gladder to see you now. I could kiss every one of you!'" Forty Mexican troops, plus one civilian, were killed in this action, while the Americans sustained two killed and six wounded, plus one man missing.

Carrizal

Towards the end of May 1916 about 10,000 Mexican government troops were massing south and west of Juarez in order to "replace" Pershing's force, who had outstayed their welcome in Mexico. The Carranza government announced that no opposition would be made to US forces retiring north towards the border, but that any troops venturing to move in any other direction would be opposed. By that time the 10th Cavalry was encamped at Colonia Dublan, where they would be based for the remainder of their time in Mexico. On June 11, trouble boiled over between the buffalo soldiers and a large group of Carranza soldiers who objected to a black trooper talking to a Mexican girl. Although greatly outnumbered and surrounded, the Americans fought their way out, killing three of the Mexicans but losing 13 of their own men taken prisoner.

Five days later an expedition was sent eastward to check on Mexican troops concentrating around Villa Ahumada. Captain Charles T.Boyd, in command of Troop C, with Henry R.Adair as lieutenant, was ordered to reconnoiter the vicinity of the Santa Domingo Ranch but to avoid contact with Mexican forces. Similar orders were issued to Capt Lewis S.Morey, commanding Troop K. The two columns converged on the evening of June 20 at a ranch at Ojo Santo Domingo, about 60 miles east of Colonia Dublan, where they gathered intelligence on Mexican dispositions from the American ranch foreman. However, Capt Boyd felt that his orders required him to take a look for himself, so the two troops rode out at dawn on the 21st for Villa Ahumada via Carrizal. (It has been claimed that in ordering this mission Gen Pershing actually sought to provoke the Carranza regime into providing the US with a *casus belli.*)

Arriving outside the town of Carrizal at 6.30am, Boyd discovered a government force awaiting his arrival drawn up for battle, consisting of three squadrons of the Mexican 2nd Cavalry Regt, estimated at "several hundred." They were deployed behind a row of cottonwoods, along a stream bed, and in the town, which was fronted by a barbed wire fence. Between the Americans and the Mexican defenses was a water-filled ditch.

The Mexican commander and his staff rode out and parleyed with Boyd, informing him that their orders were to prevent the Americans from advancing any further to the east. Boyd replied that his orders required him to pass through the town. The Mexican commander invited him into Carrizal for a conference but, fearing a trap, he declined. Both officers returned to their units; the American captain informed his troopers that his orders were to travel east to Villa Ahumada, eight miles beyond the town, and added, "I am going through... and [intend to] take all you men with me." At this, some of the buffalo soldiers cheered, and struck up "spirited songs" to show the Mexicans they meant business. Boyd gave orders for the advance; Troop C was formed on the left in line of skirmishers, with one platoon of Troop K to their right, and another on the extreme right, echeloned a little to the rear.

Corporal H.C.Houston, Troop K, recalled: "We were within 500 yards of the enemy, then we dismounted and our horses moved to the rear and we moved forward, the Mexican cavalry started riding around both flanks and when we were about 200 yards from the enemy, we received a heavy volume of fire from rifle and machine guns and we knew that the ball was opened then. We then received the order to lie down and commence firing, using the battle sight (which is the way we aim our rifles when we are fighting at close range). All of our men were taking careful aim, and Mexicans and horses were falling in all directions but the Mexican forces were too strong for us as they had between 400 and 500 and we only had 50 men on the firing line, so even though we were inflicting terrible execution, they outnumbered us too greatly [for us] to stop their advance around our right flank."

After about an hour of firing, Troop C was ordered to advance towards the irrigation ditch beyond which a Mexican machine gun section had been posted, while Troop K closed in from the right, where they were busy holding off the flank attack. Captain Boyd was wounded in the hand and the shoulder as he ran towards the ditch, and received a fatal wound in the head as he climbed up the opposite bank. Meanwhile, a squad of Mexican troops left the town and, going round to the rear of the buffalo soldiers, captured their horses.

In a situation which was rapidly becoming desperate, Lt "Hank" Adair continued to lead Troop C towards the houses of the town. Finding that his men were running short of ammunition, Adair went back to get the belts from the wounded, but during his return he was struck by a bullet just above the heart. Seeing his officer fall, Sgt Peter Bigstaff, a veteran of the Cuba campaign, went to his aid. According to a graphic (if eccentrically punctuated) account by newspaper columnist John Temple Graves, Bigstaff "fought in deadly shamble side by side with the white man, following always, fighting always as his Lieut. fought. And finally when Adair, literally shot to pieces, fell in his tracks, his last command to his black trooper was to leave him and save his own life. Even then the heroic Negro paused in the midst of that hell of courage for a final service to his officer. Bearing a charmed life he had fought his way out. He saw that Adair had fallen with his head in the water and with superb loyalty the black trooper turned and went back to the hailstorm of death; lifted the head of his superior officer out of the water, leaned his head against a tree, and left him there dead with dignity when it was impossible to serve him any more."

At about 9am, Troop K on the right was forced to fall back about 1,000 yards, with Capt Morey wounded in the shoulder. Joined by stragglers from Troop C, these men then scattered and escaped to safety as best they could. Morey and five troopers made their way to San Luis ranch, where they found a squadron of the 11th Cavalry. From there the wounded officer was driven in a motor truck to Pershing's headquarters. American losses amounted to 14 men killed, including two officers, and 23 taken prisoner, including their Mormon scout and interpreter Lemuel H.Spillsbury. The Mexicans sustained 30 killed, including Gen Felix Gomez plus ten other officers, and 43 wounded. The Mexican government troops took their American prisoners to Chihuahua town, where they were imprisoned briefly before being turned over to the American authorities eight days later.

Pershing had his *casus belli*; but although a desire for revenge for the losses at Carrizal was widespread throughout the country, and particularly among African-Americans, the US government was preoccupied with America's impending entry into the World War. Hence the 10th Cavalry spent the remainder of 1916 at Colonia Dublan, training and perfecting its equipment. The Punitive Expedition had succeeded in dispersing the Villistas and protecting US border settlements from Mexican raids, though not in actually coming to grips with Pancho Villa (who would eventually be assassinated in an ambush outside Parral on July 23, 1923). With the onset of winter in 1916, the men of the 10th were set to work building more comfortable quarters. On January 30, 1917, the regiment joined the main column in the final withdrawal from Mexico, and arrived back at Fort Huachuca on February 14, 1917.

(Continued on page 41)

Men of the 10th Cavalry captured at Carrizal on June 21, photographed in captivity; some have been stripped of their shirts, leggings and shoes. They were released on June 29, and even their horses and equipment were returned the next day – the Caranza regime was clearly anxious not to escalate the situation. (Fort Huachuca Museum)

KETTLE HILL, JULY 1898

A

UNDRESS & CAMPAIGN DRESS, 1896–1902
1: Private, Co G, 24th Infantry, c.1899
2: Corporal, Co B, 9th Cavalry, c.1900
3: Private, Co G, 10th Cavalry, c.1896

SCOUTING IN THE PHILIPPINES, DECEMBER 1899

GARRISON LIFE, 1902–1914
1: Sergeant, Co G, 24th Infantry, c.1904
2: Private, Troop D, 10th Cavalry, c.1906
3: Private, Troop L, 9th Cavalry, c.1913

D

CARRIZAL, JUNE 1916

E

FRANCE, 1917–18
1: Pfc, Co C, 367th Infantry, c.December 1918
2: Corporal, Co B, 369th Infantry, 1918
3: Captain, 370th Infantry, 1918

F

MAISON-EN-CHAMPAGNE, SEPTEMBER 1918

G

FLAGS, INSIGNIA & EQUIPMENT
See text commentary for details

1

4

5

6

9

7

8

2

10

3

11a

11b

H

Fiftieth anniversary

While encamped at Dublan, the 10th Cavalry celebrated its 50th birthday with a pageant organized by LtCol Charles Young. According to the *Army and Navy Journal* of August 12, 1916, "a non-commissioned officer, clad in heraldic trappings, recited stanzas of blank verse composed by Colonel Young, which gave a synopsis of the scenes presented. The first two episodes of the pageant contrasted the men as they appeared and drilled fifty years ago and as they appear today. The third, in which fifty troopers apparelled as Indians appeared, illustrated a brilliant feat by an officer of the 10th, Lieut. Powhatan Clark, who returned under fire during a fight with Indians to rescue a wounded trooper [in 1886]. Private [George] Wanton, of the Machine Gun Troop, one of the four Medal of Honor men of the regimental rolls [see above, 'Tayabacoa'], was the central figure in the fourth episode. He was escorted across the field of honor by a guard bearing wreaths on their saber points. The fifth illustrated the part the 10th took in the battle of Santiago, Cuba. The sixth was presented by a troop, which carried banners bearing the names of the battles in which the regiment has fought and those of its commanders who became generals. At the close of the celebration the call to colors was sounded and regimental spirit reached a climax in a great burst of cheering, ending with singing of 'Glory, Hallelujah.'"

WORLD WAR I, 1917–18

African-Americans were called to the colors once again when the USA declared war on Germany on April 6, 1917. Of approximately 400,000 African-American soldiers who served in the US Army in the Great War, about 200,000 were sent to Europe, of whom 42,000 saw combat. The remainder performed valuable service as labor and stevedore battalions within the Service of Supply. Around 367,700 of the total came into the service through the operation of the Selective Service Act of May 18, 1917 – i.e. they were draftees.

Besides these, about 20,000 were already in the Regular Army, while another 10,000 served in the National Guard of several states. However, reflecting the attitudes of that time, the War Department announced that they would not assign any of the four all-black Regular regiments to combat roles overseas because they feared that the presence of these units might cause trouble in France (the 24th Infantry had recently been involved in race riots at Houston, Texas). Consequently the Army dispersed these regiments throughout the US or American-held territory. The 9th Cavalry was assigned to Stotsenberg Camp in Luzon, Philippines, for the duration of the war. The 10th Cavalry spent the war years patrolling the Mexican border around Fort Huachuca, Arizona. In the summer of 1917 the 24th Infantry received orders to relocate to several camps in Texas and New Mexico. The 25th Infantry, stationed at Schofield Barracks in Hawaii, hoped for service in France until early summer of 1918, when they received orders to transfer to Camp Little at Nogales, AZ, for the remainder of the war.

The National Guard units drafted for the war included the 15th New York, 8th Illinois, 1st Separate Battalion of the District of Columbia, 1st Separate Company of Maryland, 9th Bn of Ohio, 1st Separate Co of

The color guard of the 15th NY National Guard – soon to be designated 369th Infantry – parade in New York City in 1917. They wear "Montana peak" campaign hats, British-style OD overcoats, and 1910-pattern canvas leggings. They are equipped with 1903-pattern infantry cartridge belts, and armed with M1903 Springfield rifles. (US National Archives)

Connecticut, Co L of the Massachusetts National Guard, and Co G of the Tennessee National Guard. When the US became a belligerent on April 6, 1917, some of these units had only recently seen service on the Mexican border in support of the Regulars.

African-American officers and formations

As the US mobilized for war, the Federal authorities showed little interest in commissioning any more African-American officers in addition to the tiny handful then serving. However, due to the campaigning of leaders such as Dr Joel E.Springarn, Chairman of the Executive Committee of the National Association for the Advancement of Colored People, Dr W.E.B.DuBois, editor of black newspaper *The Crisis*, and Col Charles Young, 10th Cavalry, a separate reserve camp was established for the training of black officers at Fort Des Moines, IA, on June 15, 1917. From the ranks of the four Regular regiments 250 NCOs were shortlisted for training at this facility, and a further 1,000 recruits were selected from the various states and the District of Columbia on a *pro rata* basis. Most of the latter came from institutions such as Howard University and the Tuskegee Normal and Industrial Institute. These student officers were put through four months of intensive training under Col Charles C.Ballou and his staff, plus a group of black NCOs from the Regular regiments.

Finally, on October 14, 1917, Col W.T.Johnson of the Adjutant General's office arrived at Fort Des Moines with commissions for 639 officers – 106 captains, 329 first lieutenants and 204 second lieutenants. These officers subsequently reported for duty at training camps in Iowa, Kansas, Illinois, Ohio, Maryland, New Jersey and New York, and became part of the all-black 92nd Div, commanded by Gen Ballou, which was organized on November 29, 1917. This formation eventually consisted of the 365th through 368th Infantry, supported by machine gun, artillery and mortar battalions, plus engineer and field signal troops. While the company-grade officers and entire enlisted personnel of this division were black, the staff and field officers, and the officers of the artillery, quartermaster, engineer and supply units were, with few exceptions, white.

The all-black 93rd Div (Provisional), commanded by Gen Roy Hoffman, was organized at Camp Stuart, Newport News, VA, in December 1917. This formation lacked a full complement of combat units and support elements, and never attained full divisional strength. Three of its infantry regiments were composed of National Guard. The 15th New York was subsequently designated the 369th Infantry, and the 8th Illinois (also known as "Chicago's Old 8th") became the 370th Infantry. Separate battalions and companies of guardsmen from DC, Connecticut, Maryland, Massachusetts, Ohio and Tennessee made up the 372nd Infantry; and the fourth regiment, which became the 371st Infantry, was composed of draftees from North and South Carolina.

African-American "Doughboys" at rifle practice behind the lines in France in 1918. (Courtesy Anne Clarkson)

During December 1917 these four regiments were assigned to the 185th and 186th Inf Bdes, and a small divisional headquarters was established, although the latter was disbanded in May 1918.

OVER THERE, 1918

The first American combat troops, black or white, to arrive in France belonged to the 15th New York of the 93rd Division. The division sailed from Hoboken, New Jersey, on December 12, 1917, aboard the USS *Pocahontas*, arriving at the port of Brest in northwestern France 15 days later (despite experiencing engine trouble, an onboard fire, and a collision with a British oil tanker). Additional units of the division arrived in various stages during March and April 1918.

When the 93rd arrived in France the situation was desperate for the Allies, after nearly four years of trench warfare and casualties numbered in the high hundreds of thousands. French Army morale had almost collapsed in 1917, throwing an even heavier burden on the British Expeditionary Force in the northern half of the 400-mile Western Front; the British had held up, but were badly weakened by their losses in the Third Battle of Ypres that autumn. With the entrance of the US into the war, the Allies breathed a collective sigh of relief and welcomed the "doughboys" of the AEF into the fray; however, there was an inevitable conflict at command level. The Allied generals wanted American formations placed at their disposal as quickly as possible, while AEF commander Gen Pershing was determined that US troops would only enter battle as an integrated and separate American army when they were fully equipped and trained. This process would take many months to complete.

Integration into the French Army

General Pershing did agree to help fill the depleted French ranks to a limited extent, however; and the troops he loaned included the four regiments comprising the 93rd Div – the French had a well-established tradition of successfully integrating units from their colonies in Algeria, Morocco and Senegal into their field armies. More importantly for Pershing, this arrangement would partially avoid the difficulty of integrating black and white American troops in the front-line trenches.

The 93rd Div joined the French Fourth Army approximately two months after its arrival in France, and served in this command until the close of hostilities. The French military trained, armed, equipped and organized the dispersed units as French soldiers. Under the French plan, a regiment consisted of three battalions, and each battalion had three rifle and one machine gun companies (under the US plan there was only

Pvt Henry Johnson, Co C, 369th Infantry, was one of the first two American soldiers to receive the French *Croix de Guerre* for bravery during World War I. The Germans made many small night raids during the 369th's first tour in the trenches. On May 14, 1918, Johnson and Pvt Needham Roberts were on sentry duty when they fought off a party of about 12 Germans using a rifle, grenades and a bolo knife. Killing four and wounding many more in desperate hand-to-hand combat, both men were wounded, and both received the *Croix de Guerre*; Johnson was also promoted to sergeant. (US National Archives)

ne MG company per regiment). For reasons of logistical commonality
he US equipment carried by the black soldiers was mostly replaced with
rench helmets, rifles, pistols, machine guns, personal accouterments
nd gasmasks; the French also provided draft horses and wagons.

The buffalo soldiers adjusted quickly to their new assignment,
ut not without some difficulties. There were problems over
ommunication (except for those who hailed from the Cajun areas
f Louisiana), monetary exchange, and provisions. Used to three
ubstantial meals a day, usually consisting of meat stew and cornbread,
he black soldiers took some time to become accustomed to the French
rmy ration of soup and bread served only twice daily.

69th Infantry: "Harlem Hell Fighters"

he war service of the 15th New York, which was redesignated the 369th
nfantry after transfer to the French Army, began disappointingly.
nstead of a posting to the front line, they were assigned to the French
6th Div and sent to St Nazaire on the western coast of France, where
hey joined black labor battalions of the Services of Supply (SOS). For
early 2 months the regiment unloaded ships, guarded German
risoners, laid railroad track, and constructed roads, storehouses, docks,
ospitals and dams. The 369th felt insulted by this "pick and shovel"
lacement, and morale suffered.

However, on March 10, 1918, the 369th were finally ordered to the
ar zone; and after only three weeks of instruction in the use of French
rms at Givry-en-Argonne, the black soldiers moved up to the front lines
1 a region just west of the Argonne Forest near the Aisne river. For
early a month they defended a three-mile sector against several
erman assaults. Although the 369th comprised less than one percent
f US troops in France, it held 20 percent of the front held by American
roops at that time.

A lieutenant and men of the
369th in a practice trench north
of Ste Menehould on May 4,
1918. They wear French helmets
and are armed with French
weapons. The sergeant
(foreground) has a Lebel
M1886/93 rifle fitted with the
50mm Vivien-Bessière grenade
launcher; he has retained his US
pistol belt and clip pouch, and
therefore presumably his Colt
.45cal semi-automatic pistol on
the right hip. The other soldiers
are armed with Berthier
M1907/15 rifles (the butt of
which was too flimsy to take the
shock of the VB launcher), and
French brown leather equipment.
At left background, one soldier
mans a M1915 CSRG
("Chauchat") automatic rifle.
(US National Archives)

After a brief respite in the reserve lines, the 369th was next placed i[n] the path of one of the German spring offensives, at Minacourt. I[n] desperate fighting the Allies finally halted the German onslaughts; an[d] on July 18, 1918, they were ready to launch their massive counter-attack[.] Thus began the Aisne–Marne offensive, which lasted until August 6. Th[e] 369th Infantry helped drive the Germans from their entrenchments a[t] Butte-de-Mesnil, and repulsed a subsequent counter-attack. By August [5] the Allies had eliminated the Marne salient and had forced the German[s] to retreat behind the Vesle and Aisne rivers.

While leading his platoon in an assault near Sechault on Septembe[r] 29–30, 1st Lt George S.Robb was severely wounded by machine gun fir[e,] but rather than go to the rear for treatment he remained with hi[s] platoon until ordered to the dressing station by his commanding office[r.] Returning within 45 minutes, Robb remained on duty throughout th[e] entire night, inspecting his lines and setting up outposts. He wa[s] wounded again early the next morning, but once more remained i[n] command of his platoon. Later the same day a bursting shell added tw[o] more wounds, the same shell killing his company commander and othe[r] officers. He then assumed command of the company until relieve[d] shortly thereafter. Lieutenant Robb was subsequently awarded th[e] Medal of Honor.

From September 26 to October 5, the 369th – now transferred to th[e] French 161st Div – participated in the Meuse–Argonne offensiv[e.] Prompted by the successful reduction of the Marne salient, the Allie[s] next hoped to sever the main German line of supply to the Wester[n] Front, destroying vital railroads and junctions, particularly at Aulnoy[e] and Mezieres. After suffering more than six hours of shelling with heav[y] artillery and poison gas on September 26, the 369th went over the to[p] "shouting like maniacs and pouring over the embankments through th[e] few remaining strands of barbed wire." Flanked by native French on th[e] right and Moroccans on the left, the 369th was met by heavy machin[e]

A soldier of the 3rd Bn, 366th Infantry, nicknamed "Big Nims," holds a British 1916-pattern "small box respirator" during a gas alert exercise at Ainvelle in the Vosges region. The British gasmask was more practical for African-Americans than some earlier French types which required wearing nose clips. (US National Archives)

gun fire and grenades. The African-American troops suffered horribly, but the survivors continued to push the Germans back 7 kilometers, until they evacuated the town of Ripont. Finally, the 369th Infantry was the first Allied unit to set foot on German soil after the Armistice, reaching Blodelsheim on the Rhine on November 18. Their tenacity and fearlessness in battle on September 26 earned this regiment the nickname "Harlem Hell Fighters." France awarded the entire unit a collective *Croix de Guerre* with silver star. Additionally, 171 members received individual awards for exceptional gallantry in action.

370th Infantry: "Black Devils"

Distinguished for being the only combat regiment to have all-black officers, the 370th Infantry, originally commanded by Col Franklin A.Denison and nicknamed by the French the "Diables Noirs," did not see action until July 1918, as part of the French 36th Div on the Meuse–Argonne front, where they manned the St Mihiel sector. On July 16, Lt Harvey Taylor received six wounds during a raid, earning the *Croix de Guerre.* During September four detached companies of the 370th served with the French 232nd and 325th Infantry of the 59th Div, taking part in the capture of the Mont des Singes or "Monkey Mountain." During these operations a platoon of Co F, 370th, led by Sgt Matthew Jenkins, especially distinguished itself by resisting enemy attacks for 36 hours while blocked in a fortified tunnel. As a result, Sgt Jenkins received both the DSC and the *Croix de Guerre.*

By October the 370th was involved in the main attack on the Hindenburg Line. On October 4 a reconnaissance was ordered to locate enemy machine gun nests in the Bois de Mortier. Captain Chester Sanders and 20 volunteers crossed the Oise–Aisne Canal and penetrated into the woods about 30 yards east of the Vauxaillon-Bois de Mortier Road. Drawing attention from several enemy machine gun posts, the patrol retired to the French lines under heavy fire and shelling without the loss of a man.

The regiment then took part in the crossing of the Oise–Aisne Cana and River Ailette and the capture of the town of Bois de Mortier. The 370th suffered its greatest loss that month while stationed at Chantrud Farm, near Chambry, when a German shell landed among a large group gathered around a field kitchen, killing 34 and wounding 52 men. The 370th had the honor of fighting in the last battle of the war, capturing a German wagon train half an hour after the Armistice went into effect on November 11.

During their combat service the "Black Devils" suffered 20 percent casualties but lost only one man taken prisoner. Although they were not awarded a collective *Croix de Guerre*, 71 individuals received the medal and another 21 the DSC.

371st & 372nd Infantry: with the "Red Hand" Division

After brief retraining, both the 371st and 372nd Infantries were assigned to the Verdun sector in early June 1918, to reinforce the much depleted French 157th Div, which used the "blood red hand" on its flags and insignia. The first combat assignment of the 371st was to fill a gap between the French 161st and 2nd Moroccan divisions. In heavy fighting, often hand-to-hand, it captured 60 prisoners, three field guns two anti-tank rifles and large quantities of ammunition. Subsequently the regiment forced the Germans from Bussy Farm and assisted in the capture of Ardeuil and Montfauxelle.

On September 28 the 371st Infantry attacked Hill 188 in the Champagne–Marne sector. As Co C led the way across no-man's-land some Germans stopped firing and climbed out of their trenches, holding up their arms as if surrendering; but as the African-American troops moved towards them the Germans jumped back under cover and sprayed the advancing black soldiers with machine gun fire, shooting down well over 50 percent of the company. Corporal Freddie Stowers rallied the survivors and, though mortally wounded, led them on to knock out the machine gun nest and capture a second trench line, causing heavy enemy casualties. His commanding officer recommended him for a posthumous Medal of Honor, but the nomination was "misplaced." Finally, after two congressmen resurrected the case in 1988, President George Bush awarded the Medal posthumously, and it was presented to Cpl Stowers' two surviving sisters in 1991, a full 73 years after his heroic death.

During the same action, Pvt Burton Holmes showed extreme bravery for which he was posthumously awarded a DSC. Wounded and with his automatic rifle seized up, he acquired a replacement weapon from company HQ and returned to the firing line, where he engaged the enemy until he was killed. The next day, at Ardeuil, Pvts Charlie Butler, Willie Boston, Bruce Stoney and Tillman Webster crawled 200 yards out into no-man's-land under heavy machine gun fire to rescue an officer lying seriously wounded in a shell hole; Butler and Boston received the DSC and *Croix de Guerre* with bronze star, and Stoney and Webster were awarded the DSC.

Of the fighting in the Champagne–Marne sector during the same period, Pvt Frank Washington, Co B, 371st, recalled: "I went over the top in the fighting on September 29 and 30. We advanced after the usual barrage had been laid down for us. We went up to the Germans, and my platoon found itself under the fire of three machine guns. One of these guns was in front and running like a millrace. The other two kept a-piling into us from the flanks, and the losses were mounting. We got the front one. Its crew surrendered and we stopped. The other guns kept right on going, but we got them, too."

Ravaged by a 45 percent casualty rate, the 371st Infantry were much relieved when their combat tour ended and they were sent to a reserve area in the Vosges. One soldier described the regiment's march from the front lines: "A dirty, tired, haggard, nerve-shattered bunch of men we were, but as we moved to the rear and the din of battle grew fainter we breathed easier and knew that for the time being at least, we were safe from the death that had stared us in the face for days. It was a quiet and somber column of men that pulled out of that sector." The 371st remained in the relative quiet of the Vosges until the Armistice. During its participation in the Champagne offensive this regiment captured three German officers, 90 men, and large amounts of weaponry including eight trench mortars, 37 x 77mm guns, 47 machine guns, a munitions depot and several railroad cars. All this came at a heavy price; the regiment lost four officers and 122 men dead, and another 41 officers and 873 men wounded. For its extraordinary bravery the regiment was awarded the *Croix de Guerre* with palm (the latter distinction marking a citation in army orders, as opposed to corps, divisional or unit orders). Additionally, three officers won the

French Legion of Honor, 123 men earned individual *Croix de Guerre* and 26 won the DSC.

The 372nd Infantry also fought bravely during the American assault in Champagne. Reaching the front lines on September 28, the regiment helped drive the Germans from Bussy Farm and joined the 369th in their attack at Sechault, where enemy resistance was heaviest. As a result, the 1st and 3rd Bns incurred such heavy losses that they had to be combined into a single unit. The 372nd next relieved the 371st at Trieres Farm on October 1, and assisted in the capture of Monthois, an important railway center and supply base. Here the regiment again met strong resistance and was often forced to repel the enemy in hand-to-hand fighting. The 372nd was finally relieved by the French on October 7; in less than two weeks' front line service the unit had suffered nearly 600 casualties, many of whom were shell-shocked rather than physically wounded.

Colonel Quillet of the French 157th Div remarked of the 372nd that the regiment possessed the "finest qualities of bravery and daring which are the virtues of assaulting troops." In General Order No.234 of October 8, divisional commander Gen Goybet informed the regiment: "In these nine hard days of battle you have pushed ahead for 8 kilometers, through powerful enemy organizations, captured close to 600 enemy prisoners, taken 15 guns, light and heavy, 20 infantry

Back in New York City in 1919, the 369th Infantry parade, "present arms" and sing the National Anthem as they return their colors to the Union League Club. (US National Archives)

mortars, close to 150 machine guns and a very important supply of engineer and artillery ammunition, and brought down by rifle fire three aeroplanes." The 372nd Infantry was awarded a unit *Croix de Guerre* with palm; in addition, 43 officers, 14 NCOs and 116 privates received either the *Croix de Guerre* or the DSC.

92nd Division: "The Buffaloes"

On August 12, after completing brief training, the 92nd Div, aka the "Buffalo Division," moved to the St Die sector near the Rhine, southeast of Metz, where they joined the French 37th Division. Two weeks later the 92nd Div engaged the enemy for the first time when it assaulted and captured German positions. On August 30 the Germans counter-attacked near the town of Frapelle, and elements of "The Buffaloes" beat them back. The following day the division repeated their success at Ormont, despite being bombarded with more than 12,000 shells in a 2-hour period.

On September 20, the division was ordered to the Argonne Forest, northwest of Clermont, where they took part in the Meuse–Argonne offensive. Due to lack of sufficient training and equipment, and unfamiliarity with the terrain, elements of the 368th Infantry failed to maintain contact with the US 77th Div on their flank, and the attack stalled. During an assault on Binarsville the next day these same troops failed to press forward and withdrew in confusion. The poor

Two of these black lieutenants aboard the transport *Ulna* wear a version of the British-style OD overcoat approved for US officers in June 1907. (Center) Lt H.A.Rogers has had his coat altered to fasten on the left; he wears a 1912-pattern pistol belt, with 1910-pattern first aid packet pouch. Both he and Lt William Andrews (left) display overseas service chevrons stitched over the "chicken guts" on their left forearms; Lt Andrews also has a wound chevron on his right sleeve. (Right) Medical officer Lt J.N.Rucker wears, over his 1904-pattern russet leather waist belt, a 1917-pattern MO's web belt with one large and one small pocket on each side. The large pocket contained a pad of diagnosis forms and a small field surgery kit, the smaller a syringe plus six ampules of morphine. (US National Archives)

performance of the 368th in September 1918 led to an unfair an completely unjustified campaign to discredit and dishonor th contribution that all African-American soldiers made to victory in Worl War I. Thirty black officers were relieved from duty and five were cour martialed; of the latter, four received death sentences, while a fifth wa given a life sentence. All five were eventually freed.

Meanwhile, the soldiers of the "Buffalo" division continued to prov themselves in battle during the closing days of the war. For example during the Allied attack on Pagny, a stronghold of the German lin opposite Metz, on November 10, two battalions of the white 56t Infantry became hopelessly entangled in the enemy's barbed wire an were being slaughtered by German machine guns. Advancing on thei right, the 1st Bn, 367th Infantry under Col James A.Moss (the bicycl enthusiast of the old 25th Infantry) was ordered to give covering fir while the remains of the 56th Infantry withdrew. In true "buffalo soldier tradition, two black machine gun companies quickly laid down covering fire which silenced the German batteries, and the 56th retire leaving a third of their men dead or wounded. The 367th held th position until relieved by reinforcements, following which the continued their advance towards Pagny. The whole white battalio would have been destroyed but for the timely intervention of the blac machine-gunners; for this action the 1st Bn, 367th Infantry was awarde a collective *Croix de Guerre*.

UNIFORMS & EQUIPMENT

At the beginning of this period the US Army was still wearing the 188 pattern uniform with various modifications. For campaign purposes, th consisted of the dark blue, five-button blouse or "sack coat," dark blu 1883-pattern wool flannel overshirt, sky-blue kersey trousers prescribe in 1884, and chasseur-pattern 1889 forage cap. In 1895, headgear wa replaced by a distinctive round-topped forage cap with sloping viso Also worn was the 1899-pattern drab or black service (campaign) ha and the lace-up brown canvas leggings introduced in 1890. The 188(pattern cork "Summer Helmet" covered with white wool cloth was issue in hot weather. The buffalo soldiers involved in the Spanish-America War in 1898 wore combinations of this clothing. Indeed, correspondent of the *Army & Navy Journal* visiting an encampment a Lakeland, Florida, during June 1898 reported that "The troops are sti sweltering in their heavy blue cloth uniforms, but it is allowable to leav off the blouse."

Canvas fatigue clothing was made available on a large scale at th beginning of the 1898 conflict, and supplemented the blue woole clothing until khaki cotton drill could be supplied in sufficient quality an quantity. Originally adopted in 1884, the fatigues consisted of a five-butto "sack coat" and trousers of 6oz cotton duck dyed brown. A Britis correspondent of the Hong Kong *Telegraph*, reporting from the Philippine in August of that year, described this uniform as "a coarse brown canva beside which our Indian campaigning dress khaki is as silk beside floc matting. The color is darker than khaki, and I think better for invisibilit but the material is altogether too much like coal sacks."

Although the khaki drill service uniform adopted by the US Army in 1898 was originally intended for officers only, it was quickly issued to enlisted men as well. Made of a lightweight yellow-brown cotton drill, the five-button blouse had flapped breast and hip pockets, and pointed cuffs. Waist belts made of the same fabric, secured by buttons at the front and supported by loops at the back, were also a distinctive feature on many of these garments. General Orders No.51 of May 23, 1898, stipulated that the collar and shoulder strap of the blouse for both officers and men were to be faced with the branch of service color. Hence, uniforms issued to the two black cavalry regiments were faced yellow, while those worn by the infantry were faced light blue. A photograph of a black trooper wearing a khaki cotton drill uniform indicates that the buffalo soldiers also had unofficial facing color on pocket flaps. This uniform, later minus facing color except for shoulder straps, and combined with the dark blue overshirt, was worn throughout the Spanish-American War and the Philippines Insurrection.

An olive drab service uniform was introduced to the US Army via General Order No.130(2?) of December 30, 1902, but issue of some old uniform items continued until at least 1904, via General Order No.122 dated July 13 of that year. Worn by the black units serving on Samar and Mindanao Islands in the Philippines from about 1904, the new uniform consisted of a blouse with falling collar and four "choked-bellows" pockets, and breeches that fitted closely below the knee and were fastened with tapes or laces. Headgear consisted of the 1902-pattern service (campaign) hat, with cord in branch of service color – yellow for cavalry and white for infantry.

In line with Army regulations, black enlisted men began wearing bronze collar disc insignia in 1907 to replace the crossed rifles and sabers insignia they had worn on the collar since 1901. The 1907 pattern called for the letters "U.S." on the right collar disc and branch insignia on the left, with the regimental number above and the company letter below. This style would last until 1917, when the

John Jefferson served in the Black-Seminole Scouts before enlisting as a trumpeter in Troop D, 10th Cavalry. His 1895-pattern enlisted forage cap rests on the chair, and he wears the regulation $\frac{1}{2}$in yellow double trouser stripes prescribed for musicians and trumpeters in 1883. An example of the sharpshooter's pin authorized in 1885 is attached to his blouse. (Mrs John Jefferson: UT Institute of Texan Culture at San Antonio, No.68-932)

Published in *Harper's Weekly* in August 1898, this photo shows men of either the 9th or 10th Cavalry as they looked during the Spanish-American War. (Right) The dark blue five-button blouse, sky-blue kersey trousers, and drab campaign hat. (Left) The khaki drill service uniform with yellow facing color, including – unofficially – on the pocket flaps. (Center) A waterproof coat of the type issued to enlisted men. (Anne S.K.Brown Military Collection, Brown University Library)

regimental number was taken off the left disc and placed below the "U.S." on the right disc.

Items of a new service uniform, consisting of olive drab breeches, overshirt, and service coat with four patch pockets and stand-up collar were issued to the black regiments serving both in the Philippines and on the Mexican Border from about 1912 onwards. Made at first of blanket wool, the 1912-pattern uniforms were worn without the coat in the summer months, until a uniform of cotton material was prescribed. Headgear began to change to the 1911-pattern campaign hat with "Montana" peak.

Due to difficulty in supplying troops operating deep in Mexican territory during the Punitive Expedition, much of the clothing worn by the 10th Cavalry was in tatters by April 1916. Regimental veterinarian Dr Charles D.McMurdo graphically described the situation in a wire sent to Fort Huachuca: "Send me a pair of trousers. Am getting sunburned." As a result of the shortage, the regiment purchased civilian trousers from local merchants in Parral. Goggles were worn by many American troops during the Punitive Expedition to protect against sand storms and glare in the Chihuahua desert.

The woolen version of the 1912-pattern uniform was worn by the African-Americans in the AEF in France during World War I. This was supplemented by the 1916-pattern shirt, 1917-pattern wool breeches, and 1918-pattern service shoes. The African-American enlisted infantry replaced their canvas gaiters with olive drab wool puttees, while the many new black officers wore leather leggings. Headgear consisted of the 1911-pattern "Montana peak" campaign hat. An olive drab wool "overseas" cap began to replace this in France in 1917, and was mainly worn in the rear areas; a branch-of-service collar disc was worn on the left side. Two slightly different styles of this cap were in use. The British version was folded in the center and issued unstitched, but the wearer could have the two ridges sewn together to produce a neater appearance. Another version with taller peaks at front and back was based on the French *bonnet de police* fatigue cap. African-American troops in France were also sometimes issued either the British Mk I, or US M1917A1, steel helmet painted a drab color. These were later embellished with painted versions of divisional patches. Most African-American units assigned to French Army formations were issued the French M1915 "Adrian" helmet, painted horizon-blue but lacking the French branch-of-service crest at the front.

Arms & equipage

By the outbreak of the Spanish-American War the single-shot, black powder, breech-loading .45cal Springfield carbine and rifle carried by the black Regulars during the Indian Wars had been replaced with .30cal Krag-Jörgensen carbines and rifles using smokeless powder. This weapon was also issued to the Volunteer regiments in the Philippines by 1901. The bolt-action, .30-03cal 1903 Springfield rifle, with five-round charger and rod bayonet, began to replace the Krag in 1904; a barrel length of 24in permitted this rifle to be standard issue to both cavalry and infantry. However, its issue was suspended due to dissatisfaction with its sliding rod bayonet. After further trials, a knife bayonet replaced this; and a new sharp-pointed "spitzer" bullet, with superior ballistic performance, replaced the round-nose .03-03 cartridge. By the end of 1906 both the 24th and 25th Infantry had received this improved M1906 .30-06 with knife bayonet. The 10th Cavalry received their Springfields in March 1907 before

The drum-major of the 25th Infantry at Fort Lawton, Washington State, c.1913, wearing the 1912-pattern full dress uniform. (USAMHI)

leaving for duty in the Philippines. The African-American combat troops attached to the French Army in 1918 were armed primarily with the 8mm M1907/15 Berthier rifle.

As to hand guns, the M1911 Colt .45cal semi-automatic pistol supplanted the .38cal revolver after the latter showed itself incapable of stopping a charging Moro warrior in the Philippines. As a stop-gap, .45cal single-action Colts of Indian Wars vintage were taken out of storage and shipped across the Pacific.

The 9th and 10th Cavalry were still armed with the US M1872 light cavalry saber in 1892, and mainly carried this weapon until it was replaced by the 1906 pattern. The 9th were issued some of the short-

Enlisted man of Co I, 25th Infantry, wearing a 1902-pattern cap with full dress facing color bands, and a post-1884 five-button undress wool blouse. (Herb Peck Jr Collection)

Cavalry trooper wearing the full dress introduced in 1902. His six-button coat is piped yellow on collar, shoulder straps and cuffs. His "bell-crown" cap has a detachable band trimmed with two stripes of yellow facing material, while yellow worsted cords and tassels adorn his chest. His sword belt, fastened by an 1872-pattern plate, supports the M1872 light cavalry saber. (Herb Peck Jr Collection)

lived 1905 experimental sabers for trial in 1906/7. The further development of the latter weapon led to the introduction of the M1913 cavalry trooper's sword, also known as the "Patton" sword after its designer George S.Patton (who saw active service as an aide to BrigGen Pershing in Mexico). The "Patton" sword was intended to be used as a thrusting weapon rather than a slashing saber; carried in a webbed khaki scabbard, it was attached to the cavalryman's saddle rather than his belt.

As they were required to serve dismounted due to the lack of space for horses in the transports, the enlisted men of the 9th and 10th Cavalry did not take their sabers to Cuba in 1898. Still officially required to take their swords into the field in 1916, the black cavalry, like their white comrades, found them to be useless encumbrances in the type of warfare waged against Pancho Villa during the Punitive Expedition, and

1st Lt Benjamin O.Davis Sr, Troop F, 10th Cavalry, wearing the 1912-pattern full dress uniform; note the crossed sabers with regimental number on his forearm below the rank knot. This officer became the first African-American general in the US Regular Army when he was promoted brigadier-general (temporary) on October 25, 1940. (USAMHI)

sent their weapons back to base. The *Army & Navy Journal* reported that a truck train arrived at Columbus, New Mexico, on April 11 carrying "a load of sabers."

The machine gun was incorporated into the US Army in 1906, a platoon-size unit being organized in various cavalry and infantry regiments. Established at Fort Robinson, Nebraska, in July 1906, the MG platoon of the 10th Cavalry, commanded by 1st Lt A.E.Phillips, developed the technique of direct overhead and indirect machine gun fire used extensively during World War I. During the Punitive Expedition the 10th Cavalry's MG Troop was armed with the over-complicated gas-operated M1909 Benet-Mercié machine rifle, chambered for the .30-06 cartridge. During World War I black machine gun units used a variety of weapons, including the French Hotchkiss M1914 and the US M1915 version of the British Vickers. Light machine guns (automatic rifles) were the French M1915 CSRG ("Chauchat"), and to a lesser extent the M1917 Lewis.

Accouterments

During the 1890s the buffalo soldiers wore woven looped cartridge belts of Mills manufacture, secured by H-shaped "US" plates; these were gradually replaced with those introduced c.1894 with a wire C-fastener. During the first decade of the 20th century the looped belts began to be replaced with the web infantry and cavalry versions of the 1903-pattern cartridge belt, featuring pockets to accommodate the five-round clips required for the M1903–06 rifles. This was later supplemented and replaced by the 1910-pattern dismounted woven cartridge or "rifle" belt. Black troops assigned to the French army were issued 1914-pattern French brown leather equipment.

Pvt Rufus Taylor, 25th Infantry, wears the cotton version of the 1912-pattern service uniform, complete with 1907-pattern collar discs and tan canvas leggings. Note the campaign bar above his left breast pocket. He has added a non-regulation sixth button to the bottom of his coat front, though it is unfastened here. (USAMHI)

Group photograph of Co A, 25th Infantry, photographed in 1913 at Schofield Barracks in Hawaii; all wear the 1902-pattern service uniform. Officers' headgear is the 1912-pattern service cap, while enlisted men wear the 1902 pattern; the officers have leather leggings, the enlisted ranks canvas strap leggings. (USAMHI)

SELECT BIBLIOGRAPHY

Army & Navy Journal (New York, 1892–1919)

Cashin, Herschel V., *Under Fire with the Tenth US Cavalry* (New York, 1899)

Gatewood, Willard B., Jr, *Black Americans and the White Man's Burden, 1898–1903* (Urbana, 1975)

Gatewood, Willard B., Jr, *Smoked Yankees & the Struggle for Empire: Letters from Negro Soldiers 1898–1902* (Urbana, Chicago & London, 1971)

Glass, E.L.N. (ed.), *The History of the Tenth Cavalry, 1866–1921* (Colorado, 1972)

Kenner, Charles L., *Buffalo Soldiers & Officers of the Ninth Cavalry 1867–1898: Black & White Together* (Norman, OK, 1999)

King, W.Nephew, *The Story of the Spanish-American War and the Revolt in the Philippines* (New York, 1899)

Lynk, Miles, *The Black Troopers, or the Daring Heroism of the Negro Soldiers in the Spanish-American War* (New York, 1971)

Schubert, Frank N., *On the Trail of the Buffalo Soldier: Biographies of African Americans in the US Army, 1866–1917* (Wilmington, DE, 1995)

Scipio, L.Albert, *Last of the Black Regulars: A History of the 24th Infantry Regiment 1869–1951* (Maryland, 1983)

Scott, Emmett J., *The American Negro in the World War* (Washington, DC, 1919)

THE PLATES

A: KETTLE HILL, JULY 1898

The 10th Cavalry was one of three African-American regiments that took part in the attack on San Juan Heights and Kettle Hill on July 1, 1898. During this action Color Sgt J.E.Andrews of the white 3rd Cavalry took a bullet in the belly. He stumbled back down the hill, still clutching the national flag, until it was taken from him by Sgt George Berry of Troop G, 10th Cavalry, who bore the regimental color. Berry then carried the colors of both the 3rd and the 10th up the slope. During the Cuban campaign the black troopers wore the dark blue pullover flannel shirt with falling collar, three small front buttons, and two patch pockets fastened by single small buttons. Dark sky-blue trousers were supported by suspenders, worn with 1890-pattern drab canvas leggings. Headgear was the 1889-pattern drab campaign hat, minus insignia – these were not authorized until July 25, 1898. Troopers were armed with M1896 Krag-Jörgensen carbines, and carried their ammunition in blue woven web 100-round Mills cartridge belts with brass wire C-clip fastening.

B: UNDRESS & CAMPAIGN DRESS, 1896–1902

B1: Private, Company G, 24th Infantry, c.1899

He wears field service uniform, which includes an 1898-pattern khaki field dress blouse with "light sky-blue" facings on standing collar and shoulder straps, as well as unofficial facings of the same color on his pointed cuffs and top pocket flaps. The legs of his khaki trousers are tapered between knee and ankle to fit inside his canvas leggings. His 1899-pattern drab hat bears "24" over "G" insignia at the front of the crown, as authorized on July 25, 1898. He is armed with a M1898 Krag-Jörgensen rifle with M1896 bayonet attached. He still wears a blue Mills cartridge belt, on which was slid a metal frog supporting a metal bayonet scabbard. His equipment also includes an 1885-pattern drab canvas haversack, and a tin canteen of what was termed "oblate spheroid" shape, in a drab duck cover. The latter was stencilled with a company letter, regimental number and individual number; the haverstack bore the "US" only, although names were sometimes added.

B2: Corporal, Company B, 9th Cavalry, c.1900

The mounted NCO wears field service uniform consisting of an 1899-pattern khaki coat with falling collar, regulation yellow shoulder straps, and five brass "eagle" buttons. His ammunition is carried in a drab-colored 1896-pattern Mills cavalry cartridge belt with C-clip fastener, supporting a holstered Colt M1892 .38cal Army revolver. His horse furniture comprises an 1885-pattern McClellan saddle,

Two unidentified African-American soldiers of the AEF. The infantryman at top has either a British Mk I or a US M1917A1 helmet, M1903 Springfield rifle, 1917-pattern dismounted cartridge belt with 1910-pattern first aid packet pouch, and a British 1916-pattern small box respirator. The man at right, possibly of the 371st Infantry, wears a French "Adrian" helmet and the US 1911-pattern OD wool pullover shirt with two flapped chest pockets; his respirator is the French M1917 ARS. (Larry Strayer Collection)

1874-pattern bridle, 1892-pattern bit, and 1896-pattern saddle scabbard to accommodate his M1896 .30-40cal Krag carbine.

B3: Private, Company G, 10th Cavalry, c.1896
The general issue field service uniform includes an 1883-pattern sack coat with five-button front and straight cuff seams, and an 1895-pattern undress cap with crossed saber branch insignia plus the regimental number and company letter in the upper and lower angles. He is cleaning his 1885-pattern McClellan saddle.

C: SCOUTING IN THE PHILIPPINES, DECEMBER 1899

This scene depicts the advance guard of a scouting expedition across the Zambales Mountains of western Luzon, conducted by Cos F, H, I & M, 25th Infantry under Capt Joseph P.O'Neil; supplies were carried by local porters. In typical field service dress of the period, some men have non-regulation flannel scarves tucked into the collars of their 1883-pattern dark blue pullover flannel shirts. They all wear the 1889-pattern drab campaign hat and khaki trousers. Two men wear the 8th Army Corps insignia on the front of their hats, while the foreground man carries a toothbrush in one of the ventilation slits he has cut in his. Some men unofficially punched their hats into the "Montana peak" shape. The sergeant is distinguished by narrow off-white chevrons pinned to his upper shirtsleeves, as authorized on July 25, 1898/September 14, 1899. They are all armed with M1898 Krag rifles with M1896 bayonets. Their ammunition is carried in Mills cartridge belts, and the rest of their equipment consists of 1885-pattern drab canvas haversacks, tin canteens in drab duck covers, and, slung on their backs, 1878-pattern blanket bags of drab canvas, to which are attached 1874–1901 pattern quart-sized tin mugs.

D: GARRISON LIFE, 1902–1914

D1: Sergeant, Company G, 24th Infantry, c.1904
The 1902-pattern full dress consists of a 1902-pattern single-breasted, six-button, dark blue dress coat, with three small gilt "eagle" buttons on each cuff. Shoulder straps, standing collar and cuffs are piped with light blue mohair. The collar insignia are the unpopular US coat of arms and "crossed rifles." The 1902-pattern full dress dark blue cap has a slightly belled crown, and a detachable blue woolen band trimmed with two $1\frac{3}{4}$ in bands of sky-blue. Above this

are pinned a one-piece cast yellow metal 1895-pattern crossed rifles insignia with "24" above and "G" below. A breast cord of light blue mohair is attached to his coat. This begins at the button of the left shoulder strap, one cord passing behind the neck and the other in front, under the first button of the coat, crossing under the right shoulder in a loop and brought together under the right arm with a slide; plited sections then pass up across the breast between the third and fourth buttons and attach to the left shoulder button, with falling flounders and tassels. Rank is indicated by three inverted chevrons of light blue facing cloth stitched to a dark blue ground. Trousers are dark sky-blue kersey with inch-wide white seam stripes. He holds a M1898 Krag rifle with leather sling, and his equipment consists of a dark russet 1904-pattern waist belt with squared bronze box buckle, supporting a fourth pattern McKeever cartridge box at the back.

D2: Private, Troop D, 10th Cavalry, c.1906
Service dress now features the 1902-pattern five-button olive drab (OD) cotton coat (exact shades varied considerably). Its falling collar displays dull-finish bronze "U.S." and crossed sabers insignia. The four front "choked-bellows" pockets are expandable by means of a concealed pleat around the pocket's edge, the pocket having the appearance of a widened horseshoe shape. Cuff seams were pointed but not trimmed with branch color. His 1902-pattern OD service cap bears "10" over crossed sabers over "D" in dull-finish bronze metal. He is armed with a .38cal M1903 Colt Army double-action revolver with cord attachment, and the M1860 light cavalry saber with 1885-pattern black leather knot, in a "browned" scabbard. His russet enlisted man's saber belt with bronzed brass roller buckle supports the revolver cartridge box and 1892-pattern holster. Footwear consists of 1904-pattern russet calfskin Blucher-style garrison shoes, worn with canvas leggings.

D3: Private, Troop L, 9th Cavalry, c.1913
Uniformed for dismounted service, he wears a 1912-pattern five-button OD garrison coat with four conventional patch pockets, and OD cotton breeches. His 1907-pattern button-type collar insignia have "U.S." on the left and "9" over crossed sabers over "L" on the right. The 1911-pattern campaign hat with "Montana" peak has a yellow branch-of-service cord and acorns. Pattern 1910 russet leather strap leggings are worn above his garrison shoes. He is armed with a M1903 caliber .30-06 Springfield rifle with brown leather sling, and a .38 revolver in an 1912-pattern swivel holster with leg strap. His belt is the Mills 1903 pattern, with 1907-pattern suspenders.

E: CARRIZAL, JUNE 1916

During the Punitive Expedition into Mexico, Troops C & K, 10th Cavalry, were defeated by superior numbers of Carranza regime troops at Carrizal on June 21, 1916. The troopers wore 1911-pattern OD wool pullover shirts, drab campaign hats with "Montana" peak and yellow worsted cords, OD breeches, and 1910-pattern drab canvas or leather leggings. They were armed with M1903 .30-06 rifles, and M1911 Colt .45cal semi-automatic pistols carried in 1912-pattern swivel holsters, with leg straps, suspended from drab 1910-pattern mounted cartridge belts.

F: FRANCE, 1917–18

F1: Private first class, Co C, 367th Infantry, December 1918

Out of the line following the Armistice, he wears service dress of the 1912-pattern OD wool service coat with five-button front and standing collar with disc-type insignia: "U.S." on the right, and crossed rifles on the left with "367" above and "C" below. The "Buffalo" patch of the 92nd Div is sewn on his left shoulder; such patches were not worn in the line, and were generally available only after the Armistice. The Pfc's rank badge is attached to his upper right sleeve only, and service chevrons to his left forearm. A brass National Guard "expert rifleman" badge is pinned on his left breast. His OD 1918-pattern overseas cap has a blackened bronze branch-of-service disc at left front. He is armed with the M1903 .30-06 rifle, and has a 1910-pattern dismounted "rifle belt." This held 100 rounds, two 5-round stripper clips in each of ten pockets; the grommets along the bottom edge allowed attachment of equipment such as the M1905/10 bayonet in the M1910 scabbard. He also carries a drab canvas-covered canteen and a M2 gas mask in a waxed cotton haversack. His trousers are 1912-pattern OD wool, his footwear 1917-pattern russet brown "Pershing" trench boots.

F2: Corporal, Company B, 369th Infantry, 1918

For combat service in the trenches he wears a 1917-pattern khaki coat fastened with five subdued "national seal" or "eagle" buttons; the bronze collar discs are blackened. The corporal's chevrons are worn on the right sleeve only. His helmet is the M1915 French "Adrian," painted horizon blue but lacking any frontal crest. Woolen puttees protect his lower legs. He is armed with the 8mm Berthier M1907/15 rifle, and he has been issued 1914-pattern French brown leather equipment, a 2 liter canteen with horizon-blue cover, the M1917 ARS gas respirator, and a cotton musette bag.

F3: Captain, 370th Infantry, 1918

His officer's service dress consists of the 1912-pattern winter cap; 1911-pattern five-button OD service coat with baler cuff braid, and four patch pockets; OD breeches, russet leather leggings with adjustable top strap, and russet campaign shoes. Rank is indicated by two silver bars on each shoulder strap; his collar has cut-out "U.S." and crossed rifles insignia on both sides. He has service chevrons on his left forearm, and wears the pattern-1906 russet leather officer's belt and shoulder strap.

G: MAISON-EN-CHAMPAGNE, SEPTEMBER 1918

The 369th Infantry advance towards Maison-en-Champagne on September 26, 1918, an action which cost heavy casualties but brought many of the 171 individual awards of the Legion of Honor and *Croix de Guerre* earned by the unit. The infantry squads making a rush towards a German machine gun position wear French helmets, 1917-pattern khaki coats with blackened bronze collar discs, and matching trousers with drab canvas leggings; the sergeant (center) has acquired a British sleeveless brown leather jerkin for additional warmth. He is armed with a M1903 .30-06 rifle, and has US web equipment; the other men carry Berthier M1907/15 rifles, plus French brown leather equipment and 2 liter canteens. They all carry British "small box" respirators in canvas bags.

H: FLAGS, INSIGNIA & EQUIPMENT

H1 Blue silk regimental flag of the 369th Infantry

H2 Field flag of the French 157th Division, with small silk US national flag attached

H3 Blackened bronze collar disc insignia, 1907-pattern, for Co H, 370th Infantry

Late 1918 & 1919 shoulder patches:

H4 370th Infantry, "Black Devils"

H5 French 157th Division, as worn by 371st & 372nd Infantry

H6 AEF 92nd Division

H7 AEF 93rd Division

H8 1902-pattern full dress cap, Troop F, 10th Cavalry

H9 1905-pattern band musician cap insignia, 9th Cavalry

H10 1915 *Croix de Guerre*, with silver star for citation in divisional orders

H11a & b 1896-pattern blue woven Mills cartridge belt worn at San Juan Heights, 1898, by trooper 62 of Troop D, 9th Cavalry

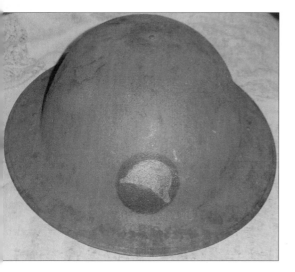

The 93rd Division sign painted on the front of a M1917A1 steel helmet. (Courtesy Russell Wolfe)

INDEX